Through her raw and honest story, Tina Booker is able to share her journey from growing up in Brooklyn, working at a prison where many people she knew ended up, to becoming an entrepreneur who helps her community as a spiritual leader. While candid and often uncomfortable at times, this book empowers people of all ages that they can do the same. With hip-hop lyrics and poetry that speak to every leg of her journey, the reader will feel like they are walking beside her as she takes you down her memory lane. Once you start reading, you will not want to put this book down!

- Patricia Wooster, CIO Designing Genius

The BLACK WILDFLOWER

The BLACK WILDFLOWER

Confessions of Love, Lust, and Life Lessons

TINA M. BOOKER

THE BLACK WILDFLOWER

First Edition 2023

TAB MEDIA AND MANAGEMENT LLC

TABLE OF CONTENTS

Introduction

"BROOKLYN RAISED ME; JESUS SAVED ME"

The purpose of my Black Wildflower series is to inspire and encourage individuals to break free from the shackles of shame stemming from past mistakes and experiences. My hope and prayer is that sharing my personal testimony with open honesty will empower you to allow the healing process to take place in your life. This involves releasing yourself from the heavy burden of guilt and shame that you may be carrying from your past. Remember, you can do it in your own way.

I firmly believe that every life has a purpose, and that God is a God of forgiveness and love. If you can't see it or understand it right now, that's okay. What's not okay is not giving yourself the time and space to figure it out. Love and forgiveness must start with oneself. It begins with appreciating who we are and fully embracing our uniqueness. The inner strength that comes from understanding your worth enables you to love, live, and, most importantly, let go.

As someone who cherishes music, I view life experiences as lyrics to countless songs. They are the written evidence that we are not alone in our journey through life's trials and triumphs. Each of us has our own lyrics to our lives, and you don't need a perfect voice to sing your song. Some of our life lyrics will have a slow tempo, filled with pain and suffering, while others will be upbeat, celebrating love and joy. This is what makes life like music for me—moments in time creatively expressed through lyrics and sound. Let the music of your life play loudly and freely.

The lyrics of my life are continuously being written as I allow God to guide my pen and set the tempo. I will continue to flow with the rhythm of my life, unburdened by the shame of my past. This is my story to tell.

Chapter 1

BROOKLYN ROOTS AND STREET WISDOM

"GO STESTA"

Artist: Stetsasonic

I came into this world on the eighteenth of December in 1972, at Kings County Hospital Center in Brooklyn, New York. My mom named me Tina, inspired by the iconic Tina Turner. Brooklyn, despite its gritty reputation, was the only place I ever wanted to call home. It was the borough where yellow taxis hesitated to cross the Brooklyn Bridge due to its reputation, a place that many perceived as violent and rough. Yet, as a child growing up there, I never saw it that way. Saying, "I'm from Brooklyn," was a source of pride for me, just as it was for many other Brooklynites.

My parents, lovingly known as "Bay" and "C-more," were not together, but they were exceptional co-parents. We lived with my mom while my dad resided across the water in Orange, New Jersey. Our lives were comfortable, always in well-kept apartments, and we usually got what we needed and wanted. My family would say I was spoiled.

My mom, who stood at a mere five feet tall, was the disciplinarian in the family. Yes, we got most of the things we asked for, but my mom was strict. I was the problem child, always getting into trouble for not listening, for doing what I wanted, or saying exactly what I was thinking, even knowing I would be disciplined. Mommy instilled in us the importance of maintaining our appearances and taking care of our belongings, especially her apartment. I would sometimes pay my younger sister, Lee, to do my chores.

My relationship with my dad was something else. He was my superhero, a tall man who was always impeccably dressed and driving impressive cars. I could confide in him about anything, and he never sugar-coated the truth, even if it hurt. I believe I inherited my boldness from him.

During my teenage years, I would often take the train to his workplace or home to get money for us. Sometimes, my sister and I even traveled to Newark, New Jersey, for hair appointments. My dad, who had street smarts from his younger days before joining the Masonic organization, shared stories of turning his life around and working hard ever since. My parents did whatever it took to make things work for us.

My little sister, Lisa, or "Lee," as I called her, and I were my mom's only children. She was my complete opposite. She was a straight-A student, never getting into trouble much and mostly doing as our mother said. I, on the other hand, was the wild, outgoing big sister, determined to show Lee all the fun that Brooklyn had to offer. But as I hit my teens, hanging out with Mom just wasn't as cool as it used to be. Still, those early days were filled with adventures with her, like our yearly trips to Coney Island and the amazing Barnum & Bailey Circus.

We have two older siblings from my dad's first marriage: my older sister Charlene and brother Teddy. I spent a lot of time with them when I was younger in Morristown, New Jersey. However, as I entered my teenage years, I preferred to stay home more and hang out with my friends.

After living in South Carolina for my second to fourth-grade school years, we moved back to Brooklyn at the top of my fifth-grade year in 1981. My mom got an apartment on Herkimer Street in Bedford-Stuyvesant that summer. The transition wasn't easy, but I quickly adapted. My teenage years in Brooklyn left a mark on me, especially during the height of the crack epidemic. My cousin Jan moved with us as well. She was more of an aunt and protected us. If someone messed with us, they had to deal with her.

Most of my dad's sisters were also living in Brooklyn. My Aunt Jo was the family disciplinarian. We all feared her. My mom would get her on me whenever I would get out of hand. We were close with her son Larry; he would look after us whenever our mothers would go out.

Brooklyn, with its extensive public housing complexes known as "the projects," was notorious for its violence. Robberies, shootings, and stabbings over money, clothing, or jewelry were not uncommon. Certain neighborhoods, like Fort Greene, Crown Heights, Brownsville, East New York, Flatbush, and my own Bedford-Stuyvesant, were off-limits if you didn't have connections or "juice," as we called it—meaning some clout or influence. Survival during that era required never showing weakness or fear.

I learned this through a few fights I had with girls trying to bully me in school the first year we got back to Brooklyn. I decided that I would fight back, whether I won or lost. Survival in Brooklyn meant learning how to stand up for yourself, and I was determined to be one of the strong ones who made it. Brooklyn had its fair share of challenges, but it was also a place of love and culture. I learned early on that what didn't break me only made me stronger.

Over the years, Brooklyn underwent a significant transformation. It's now considered one of the trendiest and most expensive places to live. However, my love for Brooklyn isn't rooted in its new skyscrapers or fancy eateries. Instead, it's anchored in my cherished childhood memories, which played a pivotal role in shaping who I am today.

Summers in Brooklyn were absolutely the best. They were filled with the music of Mr. Softee ice cream trucks, the exhilaration of playing in the spray from opened fire hydrants known as "the johnny pump," block parties, and park jams with DJs playing the latest hip-hop music and MCs hyping up the crowd. We'd engage in cheerleading and dance battles with other neighborhood kids and could even make some pocket money by bagging at the local grocery store. The indescribable scent of subway air when the trains passed underground remains etched in my memory.

Within a few months of moving to Herkimer Street, we had made friends with kids in our age group, and some older girls and guys, like Dee and Shelly, who took us under their wings. They became my mom's goddaughters, and their mothers looked out for us when my mom was working. The family of another friend, Chunk, also welcomed us with open arms.

The community at 260-280 Herkimer Street felt like one big family. Despite our occasional fights, we were united against outsiders. I always believed that having more friends meant more protection. Most of my biological family on my mom's side lived in South Carolina or Detroit. My dad's side of the family lived in Brooklyn, but I had only two cousins close to my age, and I didn't spend much time with them during my teen years. Many of the people I grew up with became my "friend-fam"—friends who were practically family. Shoutout to my Herkimer Street family and besties, including Nikay, Minnie, the twins Shelle and Relle, Takiesha and Lakishia, the Pickett, Branwell, Welcome, Fulford, and Franklyn families, along with Ms. Pat. All my homeboys from the building were like brothers.

While Nikay and I grew closer over the years, all of them were important to me during my upbringing. My mom trusted Nik's mother, Jackie, and often allowed me to accompany them to her grandmother's house in Marcy Houses. The love I felt there was reminiscent of what my own grandmother always gave me. Nik was a grade ahead and a year older than me. Our mothers were aware that we often found ourselves in trouble together.

Mommy had this knack for encouraging our passions. She made sure we got dance lessons, and I got vocal lessons. Our living room often turned into a stage for spontaneous performances in front of her friends. My love for music and dancing overshadowed any interest in school. Cyndi, a close friend of my mother, took me under her wing and showed me the broader world of African-American culture. Trips to Harlem became regular, opening my eyes to new horizons. With Cyndi's guidance, I even got to be part of a children's skit during the Annual Kwanzaa Celebrations hosted by Mr. Abdel R. Salaam, co-founder of Forces of Nature Dance Company and Dance Africa.

Being around people who celebrated their unique features, from their natural hair to their beautiful array of skin tones, helped me learn to embrace my own dark skin. Back in the day, I used to wish I was lighter, especially when I'd hear names like "Blacky", and "Black Star" thrown at me. People couldn't seem to decide if they were giving me compliments or insults, like, "You're pretty for a Black girl" or "What are you mixed with?"

I loved dressing in the latest trends, but I always added my own flair, mixing high-end pieces with unique finds. Being a New Yorker meant I was constantly surrounded by fashion and cultural shifts. Sneakers were a big deal for me during my teens. Nikay and I would shop for the latest sneakers whenever we got money from our parents. My favorites were Reebok's 54.11 Classics, Stan Smith Adidas, and Converse Chucks. I loved my Chucks because I could flip the tongue down for style, and they allowed me to dance better.

Urban fashion and style weren't just clothes; they were our way of telling stories. The more bling, the pricier the clothes, the higher your street cred.

No one was teaching us about investing for the future. Back then, it was all about the gold chains and rings, flaunting your wealth for the world to see. We followed the trends of the rappers and the local hustlers. When they rocked designer Dapper Dan outfits with Gucci and MCM logos, draped in furs, leathers, and sheepskin coats, we followed suit. Brands like Guess, Izod, Benetton, Liz Claiborne, Polo, Tommy Hilfiger, Lacoste, Sergio Tacchini, and Fila ruled our wardrobes. We only knew to "wear our wealth."

I remember only two times when my parents actually said "no" to something I wanted. My dad wasn't thrilled about me getting a sheepskin coat. He worried it would make me a target for trouble. But my mom got me that coat anyway. Dad wasn't happy, but he trusted her judgment. The Gucci boots I had my eyes on were a different story. The older girls were strutting around in them, and I wanted a pair badly. Mom wasn't sold, so she turned to our neighbor Chunk, who always dressed to impress. Chunk's verdict? Those boots wouldn't keep my feet warm, so Mom passed on them. Chunk wasn't just a fashion advisor; he looked out for us and always gave me little pep talks.

"But in the midst of all that fashion and swagger, a dark cloud had come down on our neighborhood. 'Crack' and 'dope' had crept into nearly every family." Either someone was using it or selling it. Our once tight-knit community now grappled with "crackheads" and addicts on every corner. I watched friends from my playground days change, sinking into drug dealing, theft, and a life of crime. Gunshots became an unsettling part of our daily soundtrack. Some of my own family members fell victim to the grip of crack and heroin. None of us wanted the stigma of having crackheads in our families, so we'd rather date the drug dealers than acknowledge our addicted relatives. It was a painful kind of denial, but nobody wanted to be the source of embarrassment. I sure didn't.

Respect in our world seemed to hinge on money and power. The neighborhood hustlers and tough guys commanded the most respect. My homeboy "Puerto Rican Keys," who lived in my building, taught me a lot about the street life. He became like a brother to me, and we were tight. I'd hang out with him, asking questions about everything under the sun, and he'd gladly school me. Mom didn't exactly approve of our friendship, knowing his lifestyle, but I felt like I needed to soak up street knowledge. I had to navigate those treacherous streets every day, with my dad across the water in New Jersey, I leaned on Keys and Chunk for guidance. I needed that more than her and Jan trying to protect us.

And then there was Detrick, who returned from the military and became both an uncle and a brother to us. He checked in on us daily. His protective presence was a blessing. With Chunk, Keys, and

Detrick watching over me, I didn't fear anyone. In fact, it sometimes made me a bit of a troublemaker. I'd argue and talk trash to anyone, knowing I had my crew and the boys from my building to back me up. My partner in crime, Nikay, and I found it hilarious to tease people or pull crazy stunts just for a good laugh. We played countless pranks and childish games, and even though it got us in trouble with our mothers, those were some of the best memories.

TAKEAWAY

My parents, despite not being together, were a shining example of co-parenting. They respected each other, and their primary focus was our well-being. They never uttered a negative word about each other and always came together when family time was necessary. To this day, they've kept long-lasting, happy marriages with their respective spouses. I deeply appreciate my parents' spouses for loving them and supporting us throughout the years.

Family isn't solely defined by blood. The people I grew up with became more than friends; they became family.

Chapter 2

SUMMER LIKE NO OTHER

"ERIC B. IS PRESIDENT"

Artists: Rakim Allah & Eric Barrier

Entering high school in Brooklyn at the ripe age of thirteen was both thrilling and intimidating. I was over middle school and was ready to embrace the adventures of high school life. It was the summer of 1986, a time when I began to see the world through my own eyes and no longer through the lens of what my parents told or taught me.

Growing up in an urban community, I quickly learned that our neighborhood had no time for fairytales. That summer, I embarked on my first real job at High Fashion Dry Cleaners, a Black-owned business situated on busy Fulton Street—a rarity in those days. My god-sister Dee had pulled some strings to get me the job. While my dad was initially against the idea of me working, my mom believed I needed something constructive to do. For me, this job wasn't just about earning money; it was my ticket to independence and more freedom.

Working at the cleaners meant making one hundred dollars per week, a good amount of money for a thirteen-year-old. My responsibilities included tagging clothes and operating the lottery machine, and I had to be there by 7 a.m. every morning. Little did I know, my workplace would also provide a ringside seat to the hustlers of Kingston Avenue as they sold their drugs and dressed fresh with their expensive clothes standing in front of the bodega across the street. Their daily routines became a backdrop to my summer mornings. These guys were a bit older than me, selling crack and rocking the latest style like the rappers in the music videos I watched.

Despite the illegality of their activities, my friends and I couldn't help but be drawn to these hustlers, crushing on them despite knowing we probably shouldn't. One guy, Sherman, caught my attention. He'd visit the cleaners, and I'd seen him around my building with Keys. Sherman, a fine Trinidadian with curly hair and impeccable style, made my heart flutter. We engaged in playful flirting until we both confessed our feelings. To his credit, Sherman respected my wish to maintain my virginity and never pushed me beyond a few kisses. However, when I learned about a girl he was dating on and off, I decided we should just be friends until they were completely done.

I always knew Sherman smoked weed, but he eventually became addicted to the same crack he was selling. One day, I saw him high as a kite. I felt a mix of embarrassment and disappointment, and I made the tough call to cut ties. Seeing him like that brought back all the emotions I'd had after seeing so many of the family members I'd once looked up to become addicts. They were my motivation to never to smoke weed or try any drugs. It broke my heart to watch them lose everything. Most of them eventually got clean. But, back then, as a teen, it was embarrassing.

The highlight of the summer arrived as it drew to a close during my final week at the cleaners. I was thrilled to start high school, and all my school clothes had been bought, partly with the money I earned. More importantly, I was invited by my God sisters Dee and Shelly to hang out with them and two other girls from the building Michella and Tashona. It was their way of acknowledging my transition into adolescence.

Our plan was to attend the opening night of the Union Square nightclub, the talk of the town. Hip-hop artists like Boogie Down Production, Eric B., and Rakim were set to perform, and the entire city buzzed with excitement. However, I didn't consider the potential danger of such a massive event, with people converging from all five boroughs.

The day finally arrived for me to hang out with the girls, I woke up early, filled with excitement, both for work and the night ahead. I put on my favorite cassette tape from 98.7 Kiss FM, listening to Eric B.'s "Eric B Is President." Music was my sanctuary, my confidant, and my escape from the harsh realities of life. It was my coping mechanism and my guide, even before I understood the concepts of religion or spirituality.

I meticulously selected my outfit for the night, a striking white, two-piece short set that made me feel fabulous. My permed hair hung gracefully, completing my look. However, this night would be marked by a lie—the lie we told my mom. We claimed we were going to the movies, well aware that she wouldn't approve of us going to a club. That night, we set out for 14th Street in Manhattan, where Union Square nightclub was situated. The streets were packed, and everyone seemed to be there, making us rethink our decision. The atmosphere grew tense, the police presence intimidating, and we decided it was best to leave. We huddled inside the vestibule of a residential building, hoping the crowd would disperse, allowing us to make our way back to the train station.

But our situation took an unexpected turn when some familiar guys from Brooklyn entered the building. One of them, known as "Nook," used to watch out for me in our neighborhood, often giving me five dollars for McDonald's and admonishing me to stay out of trouble. Nook was shocked to see me and inquired about my presence. Before I could respond, two white NYPD officers stormed into the vestibule, wielding riot batons. Without asking any questions, they attacked us indiscriminately. I felt a blow to the top of my head, although Nook and the girls tried to shield me.

A couple who had exited the building earlier returned to witness the brutal assault. They unlocked the hallway door, allowing us to flee inside. The officers left without uttering a word. We scattered in fear, dreading their return. Thankfully, they never came back. Then, Dee pointed out my blood-soaked shirt. I hadn't realized how badly I was hurt, but the blood told a different story. Frightened and shaken, I began to cry, and the couple who owned the building came to our aid. They provided me with a shirt and applied a compress to my head to stop the bleeding, at least until I could get proper medical attention.

All we wanted was to get back to Brooklyn. The husband hailed a yellow cab, but as soon as the driver heard "Brooklyn," he ordered us out. We attempted to seek help from other NYPD officers in a van, but they callously dismissed us as being in the "wrong place at the wrong time," despite knowing I was an injured minor. With no other options, we boarded the "A" train back to Brooklyn, ensuring I didn't fall asleep on the way home.

Upon our return, we stood at my apartment door, trembling with fear as my mom answered the door. We recounted the horrifying ordeal, and she was visibly upset after seeing my head injury. The girls, still shaken and teary-eyed, eventually left for their homes.

My mom acted swiftly, waking up my sister Lisa and rushing me to the nearest emergency room. The doctors had to shave some of my hair and stitch up the wound. Thankfully, the physician informed my mom that I was fortunate; had my blood not clotted effectively, I might not have made it.

It was a traumatic end to the summer, a night of anticipated fun that transformed into a nightmare. I was left with a bald spot on my head, persistent migraines, inquiries from NYPD Internal Affairs, and community activists using my story to shed light on police brutality. Unfortunately, there was no justice for me.

As I learned that summer, telling lies often leads to a path of more lies and disobedience. I had mastered the art of deceit early in life, using lies to shield myself from discipline, whether warranted or not. If only I had told the truth to my mom that night, I might have been spared the migraines that still plague me today.

TAKEAWAY

At thirteen I gathered some important life lessons. First and foremost, I've learned to seize every opportunity that comes my way. Dee's help in securing that summer job wasn't just about earning money—it taught me valuable skills, like how to engage with customers and the essence of responsibility at a young age.

But there's another crucial lesson I've carried with me. I watched as addiction didn't discriminate; it touched the lives of people from all walks of life.

Lastly, I learned how quickly a lie could have cost me my life. I thought that telling a lie could shield me from consequences, but as I matured, I came to understand the importance of heeding the guidance of those who genuinely care. Parents and guardians, even when their advice is hard to swallow, have a duty to protect and instruct their children. Children should trust and embrace their parents' concerns regarding safety.

Chapter 3

SKOOL DAZE

"BEST FRIENDS"

Artist: Brandy

High school was just around the corner, and after the troubling incident with the police, I was hoping for a fresh start. Originally, I was slated to attend Martin Luther King High School in Manhattan. However, my mom, always looking out for me, had reservations about me traveling to the city alone, especially after the recent events. She traveled with me the first day, mainly because she wanted to check out the school herself and ensure it was the right fit.

We arrived and found out that the principal of Martin Luther King High School had been transferred to Boys and Girls High School in Brooklyn, my mom, determined as ever, wasted no time. She requested my transfer papers, and we headed back to Brooklyn.

My mom had a plan in motion. I mentioned Paul Robeson High School to her during our discussion. Nikay was a student there, and it was conveniently within walking distance from our home. Paul Robeson was focused on preparing students for careers in business and technology, a far cry from my dreams of performing on stage. Nevertheless, my mom was determined to explore all options.

We decided to visit Paul Robeson High School, and I was surprised by how quickly things fell into place. We spoke to the guidance counselor, and the experience felt right. My mom was pleased with what she saw, and I was accepted on the spot, with instructions to start attending the very next day.

I returned the next day, I was nervous but also excited. Nikay introduced me to some of her classmates, both old and new faces. It didn't take long for me to find my groove, and I quickly bonded with a group of amazing friends.

My first friends were Shawny and Tonio. Then there were my girls Tash, Nakole, Sherla, Ang, and Yukie; we called ourselves "The Robettes." They became my best girlfriends in school outside of Nikay. I trusted them. We went through all the growing pains together. I can't forget my brothers, the "Robos," a few guys we would hang out with in school. But Robbie and Willie were my friends that I would hang out with outside of school. They were a rap duo, and I eventually became a part of their rap group. I enjoyed hanging out with them and watching their creative process. Willie and Rob even wrote rhymes for me and introduced me to a few DJs who are world-renowned these days, like Clark Kent and DJ Scratch. I eventually told them I was no rapper. Dancing was it for me.

Unlike some schools, ours wasn't a violent one, but trouble often brewed just outside the school gates. After the final bell, thugs from the Albany housing projects would often rob the students of their belongings. It was a reminder of the challenges we faced, but together, we looked out for one another. I was never robbed during my high school years. But I did get robbed one summer night on Fulton Street by two guys. They snatched the chain my grandmother bought me. I tried to chase them with some other guys from the neighborhood, but they were too fast. I was hurt because it had the gold medallion piece my cousin Mildred had given me, and she had passed away while I was in Junior High School.

As I moved through my freshman year, I found myself spending a lot of time with Shawny. I was a freshman both in school and on the Streets, learning along the way. My grades that year weren't stellar, and I had to attend summer school for math and gym. It meant sacrificing a summer vacation, my mother was strict, and I understood the consequences of not passing my classes.

It was during this time that I started to develop a unique friendship with Tonio. He had a crush on me, but I was young and didn't quite know how to handle it. At times, I was dismissive, not fully appreciating his sincere efforts. He would do sweet things for me, like bringing flowers, but I was too immature to understand the significance.

In the midst of my teenage confusion, I wasn't looking for a boyfriend at school. My attention was often drawn to the older, more mysterious guys in my neighborhood—the drug dealers and hustlers who lived life on the edge.

We were all teenagers trying to navigate life a bit too soon while desperately seeking our way out of high school. I faced the typical difficulties of adolescence. Some moments were filled with fun and laughter, while others brought heartache and failures.

Among the whirlwind of teenage emotions, I pursued my passion for performing. I joined the school drill team, a dance and singing group with Nakola, and in my junior year, we even started our own singing group called Value Pack with Shelle and Relle for a while; this was the only thing I did that was age-appropriate.

Outside of enjoying singing with my friends, my life was consumed by encounters with boys and young men, mainly from the streets. That was until the so-called "love bug" bit me, and I began to lose focus on everything else that mattered, especially my grades.

Shelle and Relle were a stabilizing force in my life, spiritually. They always invited me to church services with them. They not only sang with us, but they were also a part of gospel artist Bishop Hezekiah Walker's Grammy award-winning Love Fellowship Crusade Choir. Nakola and I didn't have as much studio experience as the twins did, but Nakola's remarkable voice made us stand out.

Shelle and Relle also had family connections in the music industry, with cousins in the popular group Full Force. One of their cousins, Baby G, allowed us to visit the studio, where we received pointers from a girl group, they were producing called Ex-Girlfriend.

With the guidance of a producer Nakola knew, we recorded our first single at a studio in the Bronx. The song was titled "If We Be Together," a sweet melody about young love. Nakola wrote it. The producer we had also introduced us to the inner workings of the music industry. He even got us tickets for the New Music Seminar, that was big for us, it was the place for new artists to be discovered.

Around the time I turned sixteen, my mom's life was also changing. She began dating a college professor named Mr. Whales, whom she met while pursuing her degree. It was a positive step forward for her, as she recognized that my sister and I were growing up. She juggled night classes after work and was no longer employed in Brooklyn. Her pursuit of an associate degree was a testament to her dedication and determination.

With my mom's schedule becoming busier, my sister and I seized the freedom we had while she was away. Our apartment and Nikay's house became our go-to hangout spots after school. Nikay's mom, a nurse, worked long hours, and our newfound freedom was both a blessing and a curse.

Unfortunately, the more freedom I had, the worse my grades became. I became entangled in the world of dating drug dealers, cutting class, and, for the first time in my life, falling head over heels in love. My grades took a serious hit, and I was spiraling into a pattern of underachievement.

Despite my academic struggles, I was well-liked in school. I was known for my influence among my peers, a quality my principal often reminded me of. He believed I had a bright future ahead if only I'd take my education more seriously. He even walked me to class on occasion, emphasizing the potential he saw in me.

However, not everyone at school had faith in me. My guidance counselor, Mrs. Speller, seemed to want nothing to do with me. She went as far as suggesting to my mom that I transfer to an alternative school, implying that I might not graduate. Some of my friends had already taken her advice and transferred out.

My mom, unwavering in her determination, firmly told Mrs. Speller that I would not be transferring anywhere. She declared, "I don't care if Tina is forty years old; she is going to walk across that stage and graduate." My mom was not playing about her commitment to see me through to graduation.

I had to take summer classes each year of high school to make up for my academic shortcomings. It was hard work, but I was determined to become a senior. As my senior school year began, I could sense it was going to be a challenge, starting with my placement in an eleventh-grade homeroom class with one of the sternest teachers in the school, Mrs. Pettus.

Mrs. Pettus didn't waste any time in displaying her displeasure, and our first encounter led to a heated argument. I simply wanted to understand why I was in a classroom for juniors when I had the credits to be a senior. Her response was rude and disrespectful, and I left her classroom, cursing in frustration.

The incident with Mrs. Pettus set off a chain reaction, and I found myself in the dean's office. Mrs. Pettus accused me of threatening her, and I received a week-long suspension. The dean's advice was for me to avoid Mrs. Pettus for the rest of the year. Although the suspension brought its own set of troubles, my mom was relieved to hear that I had officially become a senior. My counselor had to show me my transcript and place me in a senior homeroom class. But I didn't get to accompany my friends to Howard University's homecoming weekend as my punishment.

On my graduation day, as I looked around the room, I realized it would be the last time I saw most of my classmates. I proudly wore the blue cap and gown, and my family watched me walk across the stage. Even Mrs. Speller had the audacity to approach my family and say, "We did it. We got you out." I turned to her and firmly said, "Don't take any credit for me; you counted me out!" Although I celebrated my graduation with my family, it was a bittersweet day for me.

I cried throughout most of the ceremony, unable to recall the moment I walked across the stage. It wasn't all happiness; my tears represented sadness, joy, loss, and disbelief. So much had happened in my life during those four years. Check out what happened!

TAKEAWAY

Reflecting on my life, I've come to appreciate my mom's unwavering dedication as a hands-on parent. It's crucial to value the privilege of free education, something I didn't fully grasp in my youth. I realize now that many children wish for the opportunities offered in countries with free education and meals included.

We possess the ability to make choices, even as children, to shape our desired future. With focus, you can achieve anything you imagine. My high school years were eventful, and I learned to overcome mistakes and discover hidden strengths. However, I regret that my choices diverted my attention from education, costing me time and college opportunities. If I could advise my younger self, I'd emphasize the importance of slowing down and managing emotional pressure more effectively.

Chapter 4

THE BLOW AFTER SAYING NO

"LET'S WAIT AWHILE"

Artist: Janet Jackson

It was a hot New York summer in 1987. I had to attend summer school for a few weeks for not passing ninth-grade gym and math. I had no summer job. It didn't matter because it was still summertime. There is nothing like a New York summer.

I was going to do what I needed to do to get promoted to the tenth grade. Mommy always took us to Detroit for the summer to spend time with my nanny and family after my grandmother relocated to Michigan from South Carolina. I was the holdup again for our summer trip. They had to wait until I completed my classes. Until then, I made the best of the summer anyway.

I would split my time hanging out with fellas and my homegirls. That summer, I was with Shawny and Penny a lot. They both were pretty, short, and dark-skinned like me, with long hair, and they also knew how to dance. Penny was my girl from down the street on Kingston Avenue, near the dry cleaners where I used to work. We had been friends since elementary school. Her building was the place to be. A lot of the guys that would be in front of the bodega would also hang out in front of her building. We were able to be nosey and watch everything from her stoop.

Shawny lived across the tracks in the Crown Heights sections of Brooklyn, a few blocks up from the school. She introduced me to a lot of people on that side of town. Shawny and I would hang out on St. Marks Avenue across the street from Albany Housing Projects, where my friend from school, Willie, lived. Shawny was dating an older guy, even though we were only fourteen and fifteen. A lot of the guys that started liking us and our friends were older drug dealers in their late teens and early twenties, far more street-smart and experienced than any of us. They zeroed in on the innocence of high school girls, especially if their bodies looked fully developed.

They had girlfriends and children, but it didn't stop them from messing around with younger girls, which they called their "shorties." We liked the attention because they had money, power, and respect. You had to have one or all of it to survive the tough neighborhoods in New York. There was a price to pay to be protected by men like that.

That summer, I realized guys were no longer looking at me like I was a little girl. I was fourteen, the age that girls in my community began to have sex, and some were having babies, fathered by hustlers. Some of these guys were making more money than our parents. Selling crack was moving some of them out of the hood and into homes in the suburbs. But there was a dark side to that lifestyle—the bloodshed and first-class tickets to prison with their names on them. A few of my friends avoided those types of people, and I am glad they did. I should have hung out with them more.

Shawny introduced me to Kenji, who lived in the Albany projects. Kenji was known as a "booster," someone involved in stealing and selling clothing. We started dating, and I eventually introduced Penny to Kenji's cousin, Zequan. We would see each other when we could, and although Kenji would show me stolen items, I never took anything from him, my mom knew everything we owned. I didn't need to be questioned by her. We spent time together, simply enjoying each other's company, chilling, and sharing kisses. I genuinely liked him.

Soon, I began to realize that being with Kenji came with certain expectations and consequences. I observed how other girls I knew were being treated as possessions by the guys they dated, with controlling behaviors dictating their actions. One Saturday evening, Penny and I were invited to hang out with Kenji and Zequan. It was a beautiful summer night as we walked from Fulton Street to Empire Boulevard in Crown Heights, Brooklyn. When we arrived, they seemed happy to see us.

Kenji took me to a room where I was excited to spend time with him. However, I was taken aback when I saw that there was porn playing on the television. He started kissing me as soon as I entered the room, but I felt uncomfortable. He asked me to take my clothes off, which made me nervous. I expressed that I wasn't ready to have sex and made an excuse to go to the bathroom. Inside the bathroom, I paced, trying to figure out what to do. Penny sensed something was wrong and joined me. Suddenly, Kenji burst into the bathroom, cursing and swinging punches at me. Penny pulled him away, yelling for him to stop. We quickly left the bathroom and headed straight for the door, leaving in a state of panic. We walked and ran as fast as we could back home, across the tracks, fearing that Kenji might come after us. It was a long walk, but I made it home before my eleven o'clock curfew, relieved to avoid my mom's anger about being late.

I wished I had the courage to tell my mom what had happened, but I was overwhelmed by feelings of shock, embarrassment, fear, and anger. It was difficult to process how a refusal to have sex had turned into a physical assault. I didn't discuss boys with my dad after a conversation where he simply stated that it was up to me to say no. I felt that it wasn't that simple and didn't like his response.

The next morning, I called Shawny to share what had happened. She was upset and promised to talk to Kenji about it. After about a week, Kenji called me to apologize. I accepted his apology, assuming that his hormones had gotten the best of him and that he felt remorseful. Later on, Shawny accompanied me to Kenji's apartment when he asked to see me. I intentionally wore a jumpsuit that was difficult to remove as a precaution. There were a few guys chilling there, and although I was a bit nervous, Shawny's presence gave me some reassurance. I didn't expect anything crazy to happen.

During that visit, Kenji handed me two knives, jokingly saying that I could use them if I felt unsafe. I declined the knives and figured he was just being funny, but he wasn't. He once again tried to make advances, kissing me and attempting to remove my clothing. Thanks to the jumpsuit, it was difficult for him. I managed to resist and firmly state that I wasn't going to have sex with him. He responded rudely, and I immediately left the room.

I informed Shawny that I wanted to leave. Kenji and his friends left the apartment with us. As we all entered the elevator together, Kenji unexpectedly smacked me in the face and yelled derogatory insults again. Everyone around us looked shocked, and the other guys intervened, telling him to leave me alone. Although I wanted to fight back, I was scared and caught off guard. Shawny was upset, expressing that she would have never asked me to speak with him if she had known he would behave that way. It became evident that this behavior was a pattern for him.

I decided that there would be consequences for Kenji's actions. I went straight to Keys and told him what had happened. Shawny pleaded with me not to involve Keys, concerned that it could escalate into a violent situation.

Despite her plea, I told him. But, after seeing how angry Keys was, I got cold feet and never provided him with Kenji's address. After a few days had passed, I lied and told Keys that I had received an apology, and I promised never to be around Kenji again.

I cut off all communication with him, recognizing the potential danger of continuing to associate with him. I also acknowledged that my temper could lead me to act in anger, causing regrets for myself and others. Despite the traumatic experience with Kenji, it didn't prevent me from dating street guys.

I eventually started meeting and dating hustlers, including one of Keys's friends. Wade was nineteen years old. After less than a year together, I lost my virginity to him. I ended things after that first sexual experience with him. I knew I'd played myself. It was not as pleasurable as I had imagined. It wasn't Wade's fault. I just did something out of curiosity and hated it.

As nice as he was, it was over. Keys never questioned my decision to end things with Wade; he just laughed at me when I told him and Shawny what went down. That's what I got for trying to be grown. I had to laugh at myself.

My mom believed that threatening me to stay away from guys like Keys would keep me safe, unaware that boys like him were prevalent among my peers. Many of them tried to emulate older guys who had money and a flashy lifestyle, not realizing that it often led to incarceration or worse. The glorification of hustler lifestyles in music, movies, and television further influenced me.

Money, power, and respect seemed to be the driving forces. Growing up, my mom never had men around us unless she was in a committed relationship. Unfortunately, the lack of healthy relationship dynamics at home made it challenging for me to understand what a healthy relationship looked like.

TAKEAWAY

Listen up! Violence is never the way to go when someone's not on the same page as you. We all have the right to make choices that sit right with us without the threat of violence or public humiliation hanging over us. I've been there, felt the shame and disrespect, and it's crystal clear: No means No.

Life's a real teacher, and it can be a tough one. Looking back, I could've held onto my innocence; I just wasn't ready back then. Listen to those who genuinely care about your well-being. I used to watch and copy older girls, thinking they knew it all, but truth be told, they were just figuring things out like the rest of us.

Chapter 5

SUMMER OF CELEBRITIES

"MY PREROGATIVE"

Artist: Bobby Brown

Tenth grade flew by quickly. Thankfully, I passed all the state-required subject exams, and I only had one class to catch up on during the summer.

During the school year, I had the surprising opportunity to attend a school trip to see an Off-Broadway play with Nikay. Only students with good grades were selected for such activities. We were beyond excited to experience our first play, *Three Ways Home*, starring S. Epatha Merkerson from *Law and Order* and Malcolm-Jamal Warner from *The Cosby Show*.

We arrived at the Astor Place Theater, located on Astor Place in Manhattan's village area, a small but charming venue. We eagerly watched the first half of the play, and Nikay was especially thrilled to see Malcolm, whom she had a massive crush on. During the intermission, we went to the lobby to grab a snack and made jokes about how handsome Malcolm was in person. Little did we know that our humor caught the attention of the theater manager, Adele. She found us amusing and asked if we would like a job ushering for the show. Without hesitation, we eagerly accepted the offer, and it became our summer job.

Every day after summer school, I headed to the theater, often meeting up with Nikay. It was a refreshing change of scenery from our neighborhood. We were paid five dollars for each show we would usher, but the money was not the primary motivation. It was an opportunity to be a part of something different, and it kept us out of trouble, which our mothers appreciated.

At the Astor Place Theatre, Malcolm was cool and laid-back. I even had the chance to teach him a few dance moves for the opening act. We had the privilege of meeting numerous celebrities, including Denzel Washington, Forest Whitaker, and the entire cast of *A Different World*. LL Cool J came one day. He lost a gold ring and demanded the staff to find it. I didn't like how everyone was nervous about finding it and said, "Let him find his own ring." I didn't know he heard me.

After his ring was found and the theater escort returned inside from escorting him to his car, she handed me an autograph from him. She told me that he'd said, "Give this to the little big-mouth girl." We all laughed because they knew my mouth well if something upset me. Especially Malcolm.

When I wasn't at the theater, Nikay would call me and hand the phone to Malcolm, and we would joke around. He was always encouraging me to audition for *The Cosby Show*, believing I had the comedic skills for it. However, lacking confidence in my acting abilities, I never pursued it.

On one occasion, he asked me about my favorite actors, and I mentioned Eddie Murphy and Kevin Hooks. Little did I know why he had asked.

The biggest highlight of that summer was when Malcolm called and instructed me to make sure I would be at the theater on time because he had a surprise for me. When I arrived, Malcolm was waiting for me in the lobby. To my disbelief, he said, "I couldn't get Eddie, but I got Kevin." I couldn't contain my excitement. The theater staff, who were all present, witnessed the moment as Kevin Hooks, my favorite actor from the show *White Shadow,* emerged. Malcolm had orchestrated this special surprise for me. Kevin stayed for the show, signing autographs and taking pictures with us.

I felt forever grateful for what they did for me. Our relationship remained friendly and flirtatious at times. While Malcolm continued with his show and I returned to Bed-Stuy, I cherished the moments we had at the theater. That summer was filled with countless memorable moments. The theater staff even provided us with tickets to see the hit Broadway play *Serafina*, which depicted the struggles in South Africa in the 1980s. The play left a profound impact on me.

I attended a celebrity basketball game where Malcolm and the group New Edition played. Pratt Institute, a prestigious private college in Brooklyn, hosted the game, which was likely for charity. During the game, I managed to make my way into the VIP section, much to Malcolm's surprise. He didn't know how determined I could be when I wanted something. I even managed to get a few keepsakes from the members of New Edition.

A few days after the game. I learned about an autograph session New Edition were having in Manhattan that wasn't far from Astor Place. I left after work to attend the autograph session. Being alone worked to my advantage. I went with my bubbly charm and asked the security guard if there was a chance for me to get in. The line was incredibly long, and I knew the group wouldn't be there signing autographs all night.

I showed the security guard the keepsakes I had in my backpack, and he opened the door, telling me to join the back of the line inside the store. Why he did so, I'm not entirely sure, but I am grateful for his act of kindness towards me. I had the opportunity to meet the members of New Edition and have them sign my keepsakes.

I had always pursued what I wanted or believed in with determination—with the exception of acting. I struggled with short-term memorization and had a short attention span if it wasn't something I was interested in. I wasn't willing to expose myself to embarrassment again after I secretly went to an audition and couldn't remember the lines.

God was showing me that life had more to offer than just Brooklyn. I realized that I could be myself and feel safe without having to suppress my love for the arts. The theater staff, with their diverse backgrounds and lifestyles, taught me that people are people, regardless of their differences.

TAKEAWAY

Seize every opportunity and make the most of it. These experiences become great stories to share and bring joy on days when things aren't going so well. Growing up in a community where violence and drugs were prevalent, it wasn't easy to avoid those influences. My summer job at the theater showed me that opportunities are endless when we take them.

Chapter 6

LESSONS AND LOYALTY

"JUST GOT PAID"

Artist: Johnny Keep

Every year we had something to look forward to—my grandmother, whom I affectionately called "Nanny," was visiting from Detroit for the Thanksgiving holiday. Her cooking was unmatched.

After school one day, I saw Keys sitting on the stoop in front of our building. My grandmother had asked me to run a few errands that day, but I decided to first hang out with him for a bit before heading to the store for her.

Suddenly, a gunshot rang out, and Keys instructed me to get down. Two men with Jamaican accents and dreadlocks were yelling and firing shots in our direction. Miraculously, we survived, but Keys got shot in the leg. Despite his injury, he cared more about my safety.

We made it to his apartment, where the reality of his street lifestyle hit home. I felt a mix of fear and concern for Keys, and the need to process the situation. Keys asked me to inform his friends about the incident, which I did before getting those errands done for my grandmother.

This incident showed me the dangers of being around someone involved in street life. Despite his lifestyle, Keys treated me like a sister, and our bond grew stronger. I remained loyal to the people I loved, and Keys knew he could count on me.

During his recovery, I continued to support him, running errands and ensuring he had what he needed. After that incident, hearing and reading about shootouts were almost the norm.

During school's winter break in 1988-89, I had finally turned sixteen during my Junior year, I attended a New Year's Eve party in Brownsville, Brooklyn. Chunk's aunt, Avia, had invited us to her boyfriend's party. I went with Lakishia.

At the party, I met a guy named Deez. He expressed his interest in me and asked Avia's boyfriend if he could dance with me. Initially, I refused, but her boyfriend assured me that Deez was cool and encouraged me to dance with him. Being in Brownsville for the first time, I noticed that the guys there were different from the ones I was used to in Bed-Stuy. They carried guns in the back of their jeans or at their waist. Brownsville had a reputation.

We danced to a song by Keith Sweat, "Right and Wrong Way". I'd never slow-danced with a guy that seemed so tough before. After dancing with Deez, he told me he was interested in me. I revealed my age, sixteen, expecting him to say I was too young. However, he responded with, "It ain't the age, it's what's on stage," which I found amusing. We exchanged numbers, and that night marked the beginning of our relationship. He was twenty-two.

I would occasionally cut school and take taxis to meet him in Brownsville. I would meet him at a check cashing spot sometimes. He would be there collecting his money owed by those strung out on crack on their check days. I knew he was a crack dealer, and people feared him.

Despite the risks, I liked being with him watching how he controlled everything and everyone around him. We would talk about everything. If I couldn't make it out to Brownsville to see him, he would send money to my house by a guy who hustled for him. I would spend the money on junk and lunch for my friends. Again, knowing my mother would have picked up on it quickly if I had brought anything new home that she didn't buy.

After dating Deez for a while, we became intimate, and it was a completely different experience from my first time. I wasn't in love with him; there were no emotions involved for me. I felt comfortable and not forced. It was like we had a routine. I'd cut school. He would take me to hotels and tell me about his day. They always seemed stressful and dangerous. He would fall into a hard sleep for hours, probably from hustling all night.

I would sit and watch my favorite video show, *Video Music Box*, until it ended, signaling it was time for me to head home and act as if I had been in school all day. He would call me a cab, pay them, and give me money for my pocket. He always called to make sure I made it home safely.

While still in the eleventh grade, my girl Nakola introduced me to a non-profit youth organization called City Kids Foundation. It was a mentoring, creative, and performing arts program for teens and young adults, with support from the artist Keith Haring. Located in lower Manhattan, Nakola kept inviting me to join her one Friday. Although I usually cut school to spend time with Deez in Brownsville, that routine started to get old. I became more focused on singing, the drill team, and dancing with Nakola.

City Kids had an all-male hip-hop dance group called the "IBM Dancers," and Nakola had started dating one of the dancers. They were looking for female dancers, so I decided to accompany her the following Friday. I knew I was a good hip-hop dancer, having won numerous local battles and competitions in my neighborhood. To be selected as one of the female dancers for IBM, I had to audition, which I was confident about.

On Friday, we headed to City Kids for auditions. When we arrived, the group of guys, eight of them, were already showcasing their impressive dance skills. I was amazed by their techniques; they were unlike anything I had seen before. Nakola didn't audition since they were already aware of her skills. It was finally my turn to show what I had, and although I don't recall how many I competed against, they were thoroughly impressed with my dancing and offered me the only available spot. They were only looking for one girl, as Nakola was already part of the group. I was ecstatic because we were already a dance duo.

Years later, one of the dancers revealed that the competition was initially fake, designed to attract girls. However, once they witnessed my talent, everything changed. My dance name was "Shakie," and interestingly, I had been doing the dance now known as the "Harlem Shake" decades earlier.

After winning the challenge, we invited IBM to perform at our high school's drill team talent show. They accepted, and the guys were starting to get more performing gigs at various high schools. I began bringing some of my friends to City Kids, just like we did when we worked at the Astor Place Theatre. The guys in IBM lived in Brooklyn, so we would travel home together each week. I started to like one of the dancers named Mel, his stage name as a dancer was "Show", even though they had many girls interested in them and were dating multiple girls in the program.

At the talent show, Nakola and I performed as a duo for the first time on stage as IBM's female dancers. We danced to De La Soul's "Me, Myself, and I" and incorporated some of the guys' moves into our routine. We were proud of ourselves, and the guys' performance had the audience going wild. IBM was truly making an impact.

We were all on cloud nine after our performance that night. We decided to hang out at Nikay's house since her mom was working overnight at the hospital. My mom allowed me to spend the night there, and eventually, everyone ended up staying over. We played games, sang songs, and had an unforgettable night of fun.

That night, Mel confessed that he liked me. He was the one who had captured my attention from the first day I met the group. He was an incredible dancer. I liked everything about him, and we flirted with each other during rehearsals. I couldn't help but wonder where he had been all my life. He could have been my Patrick Swayze from *Dirty Dancing* or my Channing Tatum from *Step Up*.

Mel and I spent the entire night talking, kissing, and sharing stories about our lives and families. Deez was the last thing on my mind when Mel asked me to be his girlfriend. I was honest with Mel and told him everything about Deez. He was concerned about how I would break up with a drug dealer. I assured him that I would handle it, and I did.

The next day, I called Deez and explained that I no longer wanted to be with him. He asked why and if he had done something wrong, but

I assured him that he hadn't. I simply found someone my own age who shared my passion for dance. I mentioned that our relationship wouldn't have gone far anyway, as it was just another case of the same story with a different player. Although he wasn't happy about it, I didn't let it bother me. A few minutes later, he called me back, but I reiterated my decision and thanked him for being good to me. We hung up, and I never contacted him again.

After ending things with Deez, it was all about Mel and me. We became "Shakie and Show." I remember taking my denim jacket and graffitiing our names on it. I made sure to wear it to City Kids, letting all the girls know that he had chosen me as his girlfriend.

TAKEAWAY

Reflecting on this chapter of my life, it's evident that the choices we make in our youth can introduce us to unexpected partners and passions. It's not solely about being carefree; it's about exploring, learning, and seizing opportunities.

My love of dance introduced me to my first love and removed me from a relationship with someone I never should have been with or around at my age. I was happy to finally stop hiding a relationship and being with someone I could finally introduce to my mother as my boyfriend.

Chapter 7

TEENAGE LOVE

"ALL I WANT IS FOREVER"

Artists: James "JT" Taylor & Regina Belle

I was filled with excitement and anticipation whenever Mel and I were together. Every moment felt special. One day, he invited me to dinner to meet his family. His mom had a warm and instant connection with me. I was surprised to find out that she shared my dark skin tone and slim figure. In my eyes, he was a lighter-skinned version of his mother. Both of our parents approved of our relationship, and they would communicate to ensure our safety when we visited each other's homes.

Mel had a wonderful sense of humor that always made me laugh. It was then that I truly understood what my friends meant when they talked about being in love. I had never experienced those intense emotions before. We spent the summer of 1989 and most of my senior year together. I loved Mel with all my heart, and being intimate with him only deepened our connection. It wasn't just about physical pleasure; I wished I had saved myself for him.

I dreamed of marrying him and spending the rest of my life by his side. Thoughts of him consumed my mind. Meanwhile, my sister started dating one of the dancers, Boogie. Once I discovered their relationship, we all became even closer. Mel along with his best friend and fellow dancer Chancey Also spent a lot of time at our apartment with him and Boogie.

After almost a year of dating, and as the guys gained popularity in the dance circuit, Mel and I started growing apart. During the second half of my senior year, rumors began circulating about him cheating on me with different girls. Although he always denied it, my jealousy intensified whenever I saw him talking to other girls. Unfortunately, I allowed my temper to overshadow my talent, and I became known for my anger at City Kids.

I still remember the first gift he bought me—a designer wallet with the money he earned from appearing on the soap opera *One Life to Live*. Mel quickly started making money through dancing and began buying things for himself. I never asked for anything; all I wanted was him.

Eventually, the group got a manager named Marico, who kept them busy. He booked us for a music video with a rap artist I had never heard of before. To this day, I still don't know who it was, as they didn't make it far in the hip-hop scene. Mel wasn't entirely innocent; he was flirtatious and commanded attention whenever he danced. He had undeniable star power.

On the day of the video shoot, we arrived early to practice. However, Mel and I started arguing when we were paired up. We had always had great chemistry on the dance floor, but during this time, our arguments became more frequent. He knew how to push my buttons, and he kept acting like I was messing up the choreography. I felt he was doing it to be paired with one of the hired girls who weren't part of our group, just to shine more.

Marico had enough of our arguments, and my temper got the best of me. I started cursing loudly at Mel, and Marico decided that we could never be dance partners or work on projects together again. At the time, I didn't fully grasp the consequences of his decision other than the fact that we couldn't dance together. It was only later, as time passed, that I understood it marked the beginning of the end for me dancing with the group.

The video shoot for the unknown rapper got canceled anyway, which left us feeling disappointed after weeks of preparation. However, Marico found out about another video shoot happening nearby and offered us the opportunity to be in it without auditions. It was a chance for me to calm down and regain my composure.

When we arrived at the location, I couldn't believe who was shooting the video—it was one of my favorite rap groups, Boogie Down Productions. They were filming the video for their song "You Must Learn." I was starstruck. The same group I had wanted to see perform on the night I was assaulted by a police officer was now giving me the chance to be in their music video. The day ended on a much better note for Mel and me. I even had the privilege of meeting some of my favorite hip-hop artists, including Queen Latifah, D-Nice, and KRS1. It was a long day of shooting, but they treated us well.

A few weeks later, City Kids hosted their annual fundraising event at the Jacob Javitz Center in Manhattan. It was a Saturday afternoon, a day that brought me both happiness and pain. I was excited to see everyone. The event aimed to raise money for City Kids, and Marico kept his word we weren't asked to participate. It became clear that the fellas were the main focus, and us girls were just an addition that didn't fit well.

We were gradually removed from the group without anyone explicitly saying it. We were no longer asked to perform, only invited to support. I attended the event with my sisters, Lee and Penny. The guys had their own dressing room. We were told to wait there until they performed.

Mel briefly entered the dressing room before their performance and gave me a kiss, but something felt off. After their performance, Mel never returned to the dressing room. I decided not to wait for him and asked them to tell him I was leaving. Once we left, I realized I had forgotten my handbag.

As I headed back down on the escalator, I saw Mel at the bottom, talking to a girl. It confirmed the rumors I had heard. He was leaning into her, and their eyes were locked. When he saw me, he couldn't say a word. I had witnessed other guys getting caught by their girlfriends before, but I never thought it would happen to me, especially at an event he knew I would be attending.

I had shed countless tears before, fearing that the rumors I heard might be true. As usual, my pain transformed into anger, leading me to respond with threats and curses toward him. Both Penny and my sister were present, witnessing the whole ordeal.

Penny tried to console me, repeatedly saying, "Forget him, Tina, he's not worth it." The pain I felt was unlike anything I had experienced before. Chancey empathized with my situation. I knew Mel was still his best friend, so he couldn't betray him. He walked alongside us, ensuring I stayed away from Mel as we made our way to the train station. On the other side of the street, Mel walked with the girl, displaying no regard for me or my feelings.

Since they prevented me from fighting, I did everything in my power to embarrass him in front of her. My heart was shattered. Chancey made sure we got back to Brooklyn safely.

By the time I got home, Mel's mom had called my mom to check on me because she overheard Mel and Chancey talking in the room. She knew he had done something wrong to me and wanted to speak to me and hear what happened. I told her everything, and she informed me that he was very upset about it. She convinced us to talk on the phone. She put him on the line, but I didn't want to be nice. I wanted him to hurt like I did.

I started bragging about another boy from my neighborhood named Johan, who liked me. I made sure to mention how well he dressed and his gold teeth. Mel didn't have much until he started making his own money, so I knew it would hurt him.

I told him how Johan walked me home from school and was waiting for me to break up with him. It was all true, but despite Johan's kindness toward me, I never cheated on Mel. Once I said those things, he got angry and had the audacity to say he hated me. I knew he was just speaking out of anger.

He knew the type of guys I had dated before, and he knew they were nothing like him. He was right; I wanted to go back to dating street guys with money. If my heart was going to be broken, I wanted it to be by someone who took care of me, at least as I saw it in my mind back then.

Chunk always told me not to give up something for nothing and to know my worth. After that day, I would hear even more rumors about Mel cheating on me with other girls. We continued the cycle of making up and breaking up. His mother even showed me a picture of a girl he was staying with in Harlem. He wasn't even going home anymore. The heartache was unbearable, and I cried every day whenever thoughts of him crossed my mind.

My friends tried to cheer me up, but nothing they did could mend my broken heart. I decided to date a few guys who liked me, especially Johan. He knew about Mel but didn't care. He believed the best man should win. I didn't become intimate with any of them. Nobody warned me that you couldn't just shake off love.

My heart was fully invested in Mel. Every time he came back around, I would stop talking to the other boys. Johan was the only one I considered a friend. I grew closer to him, especially after he got shot in both legs during my senior school year. I rushed to the hospital to be there for him, and once I knew he would be okay, I continued to check in on him while focusing on getting out of school.

The thought of losing him made me value our friendship even more. Trying to cope with heartache and school was no easy task. Even seeing Boogie when he came to see my sister made the pain worse. I tried to stay away from home as much as possible.

I knew the dreams I had for Mel and me were over. We had become two teenagers who didn't know how to let go of what we'd thought was love. He knew exactly what to say to draw me back in, but it took me a while to learn to reject him.

TAKEAWAY

I learned the hard lessons of love and heartbreak. These experiences, etched into my memory, taught me that healing comes when we allow ourselves to move on, even amid uncertainty. At sixteen, I realized I'd invested too much too soon in a relationship. It's crucial for young people to understand themselves and take time to process emotions rather than rush into another bad situation to numb the pain.

Chapter 8

BITTERSWEET DECISIONS

"ALL CRIED OUT"

Artist: Lisa & Cult Jam

I was happy the school allowed me to go on my senior trip. During the trip and afterward, I started experiencing severe migraines and nausea, worse than the ones I had after my incident with the police. I felt terrible on some days and noticed that I hadn't gotten my period, which had never happened before.

I confided in my friend Ang, and we decided to take a pregnancy test, which turned out positive. The thought of my mother finding out terrified me, and I immediately chose to have an abortion. I didn't want to bring any more trouble home; it always seemed to revolve around me. The only thing on my mind was dealing with my mom's reaction and having a baby with a cheater.

When I told Mel about the pregnancy, he revealed that his family didn't believe in abortions and wanted me to keep the baby. We argued about it every day, but I had made up my mind. With Ang's support, I searched for assistance to have an abortion. Although I was scared, I knew I couldn't handle having a baby at that time, especially since I had just turned seventeen and trying to graduate.

One Saturday afternoon, my mom walked into my room and asked if I was pregnant. I burst into tears and admitted it. She asked me two more questions: did I want to go to college or have a baby? I responded that I wanted to go to college. I think my sister told her. After my response, my mom didn't say a word and walked away. The pressure felt overwhelming. I couldn't stop thinking about how I was embarrassing my family and dealing with a broken heart. At seventeen, making a decision that would change my life was not easy. I had friends who already had babies, but I followed my instincts, even if I didn't know if I was making the right choice.

Days passed, and my mom arranged an appointment for the procedure in New Jersey. We took a bus there. The room where the procedure took place seemed huge, dark, and cold.

I was trembling and nervous, feeling utterly alone. My mom stayed in the waiting area, leaving me without anyone to hold my hand through another traumatic experience. As always, I sucked it up; it was my problem, my pain. After the procedure, I got dressed, and we headed home. I felt weak and tired from the anesthesia. We never spoke about it again. I was emotionally drained.

When I told Mel over the phone, he threatened to tell his mother what I did. He never considered my feelings despite everything he had put me through. At that point, I didn't care who he told, and he knew it.

I returned to school as if nothing had happened. I humbled myself and apologized to my teachers, who thankfully allowed me to make up for my missing schoolwork. The physical education director, Mr. Spielberg, looked out for me the most. I had three gym classes to pass in order to graduate, and I passed all of them except one.

I explained to him the truth about what I had gone through and how I couldn't do the strength training in that class while healing.

He agreed to pass me after seeing my commitment in the other two classes. I cried tears of gratitude in his office; I was so thankful.

My heart had been broken, my body traumatized, and I had faced adult situations as a teenage girl. The life I had known for the past four years was about to change completely. It was time for new beginnings, and I knew I could heal along the way. I was headed to visit my family in Detroit, ready to enjoy my accomplishment and celebrate graduating.

TAKEAWAY

Navigating my senior year was like trying to find my way through a dark, winding tunnel. The weight of a secret, an unexpected pregnancy, hung heavily on me. Fear of judgment and shame clouded my every thought. But I made a choice, one that was right for me at the time. It wasn't easy, but I knew I needed to prioritize my education and future. Graduating high school was a bittersweet victory, symbolizing the end of one challenging chapter and the start of new beginnings. It was a journey of growth, learning to stand up for myself and realizing that sometimes, the hardest decisions are the ones that lead us to brighter tomorrows.

Chapter 9

GOTTA MOVE ON

"KEEP ON MOVIN"

Artist: Soul II Soul

I arrived in Detroit and stayed at my nanny's brick home on the west side. My grandmother lived upstairs, while my Aunt Ruddie and her three children lived downstairs. Aunt Ruddie and my grandmother always allowed my cousins' friends to hang out on the porch with us. My grandmother took care of all the kids.

My cousin Kendra, whom we called "Ken," had just graduated and was heading to college. To celebrate, the family threw a big barbecue for us. Nanny took me shopping for a graduation gift, and I chose the gold chain that I got robbed for about a year later.

Ken had a car, and we had an unforgettable summer together. We went to parties and concerts and spent time at Belle Isle and River Rouge Parks. We even attended a hip-hop concert to see the rap group Naughty By Nature.

I even met a boy! His name was Ronny, also known as "Riz." We had a summer fling, and I enjoyed his company every day. During that time, I didn't think about Mel.

My sister Lee returned home with our mom, but I stayed in Detroit. We spoke on the phone, and she mentioned that Mel missed me and wanted to see me. However, I focused on spending time with Riz and my family before heading back to Brooklyn. Ken traveled back with me to visit her dad in New Jersey before school started. A few days later, Mel called. He wanted to meet up, saying he missed me and wanted to see Ken. He invited us to his mother's barbecue, and I agreed to go.

Everyone was happy to see me at Mel's house, but he kept trying to hug and kiss me, asking if I missed him. I kept pushing him away, not wanting to let my guard down. Something about being with Riz and getting closer to Johan gave me the strength to resist him. Mel kept telling me he loved me and was hurt that I terminated my pregnancy, but I didn't believe him.

Mel's mom, Mrs. Wanda, pulled me aside and told me she loved me like her own daughter. She gave me money as a graduation gift and said she wanted me to do something great with my life.

She then mentioned that a girl had been claiming to be pregnant by Mel. My heart sank, and tears filled my eyes. Mel came back, and he started yelling at his mom, asking what did she say to me. When she confirmed that she had told me about the girl's pregnancy, Mel grabbed me, denying it. But I knew his mom wouldn't have told me if she didn't believe it.

Once again, I was subjected to Mel's hurtful behavior in front of my friends and family. But this time, I refused to make a scene. I asked him why he would disrupt my life, knowing what he had done.

Tears streamed down both our faces as he tried to explain, but I couldn't hear anything after that. Mel's tears weren't about my feelings. They were about him knowing he had gone too far, and I wasn't going to stay around for it anymore.

With his popularity and all the girls he too had access to as a hip-hop dancer, I knew Mel would never choose just me. He'd also gotten someone else pregnant at the same time as me. I was done.

I told him I had to go, gathered everyone, and left. I didn't even let him walk us to the train station. Back at my apartment, I confided in Ken. She knew I was hurt and supported me. We listened to music, I found comfort in the melodies. I had already been talking with Johan, and I knew we liked each other. After the baby news, I was certain it was over with Mel.

I decided to move on and enjoy the rest of my summer with Johan. He needed me as he healed from being shot, and I needed him to heal my heart. Johan and I became a couple, while Mel became a father after all.

TAKEAWAY

Staying with my family brought me joy. Adventures with Ken created unforgettable memories, and meeting Riz offered a temporary escape from my past. Confronting Mel showed me the importance of prioritizing myself.

That summer was filled with ups and downs, but it taught me valuable lessons. Stop looking back to something that's not there. The love was gone.We go through so much and forget that even in the midst of heartache, there is always room for healing and new beginnings. When you're young, push as hard as you can to not stay stuck on one thing. Give yourself new hope for happiness.

Chapter 10

COLLEGE BOUND

"NO BONES IN ICE CREAM"

Artist: Nice and Smooth

College was actually in my future! My mom's boyfriend, Mr. Whales, was able to pull some strings at State University at Old Westbury in Hicksville, New York, for me to do late registration.

I passed the entrance exam. I guess I was smarter than I knew I was. I had heard about Old Westbury. It was known for being a party school. A lot of kids from Brooklyn would go to the parties on the campus. Knowing I had a college to attend made enjoying the summer even easier.

It was time for me to travel to Long Island. A backpack kid from Brooklyn, I always had my Walkman with me to listen to my music during my commute. Although the school was in New York, it felt like I had gone far away. The majority of students at Old West were Black or Hispanic. I was happy they offered degrees in media and communications. Finally, some form of education that spoke my language: entertainment and the arts. I chose that as my major. I always said I wanted to be the Oprah of radio. I wanted to have a career in music and some form of journalism. Due to my grades in high school and low SAT scores, I had to take English and math remedial classes my first semester. Math was my problem. I just could not grasp it. Truth be told, I still can't, especially if it doesn't equal money.

My homegirl, Lakishia, decided to attend the same school when she found out I was going. We did almost everything together anyway. She chose to stay on campus. I didn't; it was too expensive for me at the time. My dad spent the money he had saved for me to go to college. He said he didn't think I would even go to college as much as I hated school. He only gave me sixty dollars a month to commute. I had my classes set up for Mondays and Wednesdays from 2 to 6 p.m.

Lakishia's roommate didn't mind me staying with them most of the time. This gave me free time to get back to Brooklyn.

Although I was enjoying my first semester of college, I still wanted to run home on my days off to Brooklyn to be with Johan and my friends. His mom, Mrs. Sherry, would allow me to come to their apartment even if Johan wasn't home. She would cook the best food. I'd watch TV with his baby brother Boo. Johan was the oldest of four. His brother Franklin was my homegirl Ekiah's boyfriend. His sister Treecie, being the only girl, was a little firecracker. She was like a little mama; I would laugh listening to her tell everybody off.

Johan would ride with me on the handlebars of his bike to make sure I got home safely. He would be cracking jokes on people all the time. He loved a good party, like I did, and he was a fighter, never letting anyone bully him.

Though he was flirtatious, like Mel, I never felt like he would deliberately try to hurt me. He would hang around girls in the park but came to me whenever I showed up to reassure me it was all about us.

On the weekends, he would come with me to pick up my cousin Jan's kids to give her breaks. They were our babies also. We'd drop them off to family that lived on his block: Aunt Elly, Leza, and Neeka. We were all close.

Being from the same neighborhood was cool because we both knew the same people, and they knew we were together and wanted us to be. Especially my friends after what I had recently been through.

Spending all those late nights at Johan's house landed me in another situation. I was pregnant again. I was mad at myself. I had been so irresponsible, knowing what I had just gone through less than a year before.

This time, I was going to keep the baby because Johan treated me so well. I figured I would have the baby and finish school. I called Johan and told him the news. His response was different from Mel's. He didn't want the baby. He didn't even seem like the same person. He started avoiding me or dismissing the conversation. He said his mother would kill both of us. I started making plans to become a single mother. I was so upset and told him I didn't need him. After how I supported him, he was abandoning me. I told a few of my friends and even avoided taking the required MMR vaccine for school because I was pregnant. I was well over two months and still had to tell my mother. I knew she would be disappointed and angry after all she had done for me. She had every right to be.

After a while, it weighed on me that I would have no support, so I made the decision to give Johan what he wanted and hide my shame again. I didn't want him to hate me or our parents to look down on me. I felt like a total failure.

The decision to terminate again broke me emotionally. I asked myself, why did I let my emotions and love for someone cost me so much?

I was angry. I made an appointment at Planned Parenthood. I told Nikay I needed money to pay for it and I needed to have an escort. I spent the night at her house; she took the savings she had inherited and gave it to me. That's my sister for life! I was so scared and torn.

I wanted my baby, but I knew mentally I couldn't handle the rejection from Johan and our families. The social workers were discussing my case outside the office where I was waiting. This woman came back into the room and read me my rights as if she were my mother.

She asked, "Where is this boy who got you pregnant?" I told her the situation. She told me to take my life seriously and that she didn't want to see me back there again in this same situation, especially without support from the father.

She further explained that I would not be able to get the procedure done in one day. I was already almost in my second trimester, and I would need a two-day procedure. I had no idea what that meant. I just got even more nervous. She told me what they were going to do, and I had to come back the next day for them to complete the procedure. I acted as if I understood everything.

I signed the papers and went inside for them to begin. The palms of my hands were sweating, and my heart was beating so fast. The medical staff laid me down, but I wasn't put to sleep.

The pain I experienced was indescribable. After everything, the nurse gave me instructions and told me I had to return at the time they gave me for the next morning, and if I didn't return, I would miscarry and begin to hemorrhage. Nikay was my escort, and I spent the night at her house again.

I was too scared to fall asleep, thinking I may die. We got up early and returned as instructed. It was too late to change my mind. I finished what I started. Nikay made sure I got home. My sister was at school, and my mom was at work. I still had to get my prescription filled, so I took the B25 bus on Fulton to the Rite-Aid across from Brevoort housing projects. I was too scared to go to the drugstore across the street from me. I thought someone would see me in all my shame. I resented Johan. I saw him when the bus passed, standing on the corner. I got home and called him; he answered the house phone, and I told him I was no longer a problem for him. I hung up, not giving him a chance to speak. I cried my eyes out after. I got myself together before anyone came home.

For two months, I ignored his phone calls. But then, around mid-November, I finally decided to talk to him. As hurt as I was, I had to forgive him after he told me he had been scared, and he was sorry he didn't support me out of fear. He told me he wished I would have ignored him and did what I wanted because he would have done the right thing. I told him I couldn't assume he would have and had to make the hardest decision to do something I didn't want to do.

I still cared for him, and our families loved each other too much for us not to be connected in some way, but I knew we could only be friends going forward. Johan didn't know what had happened months prior with Mel or all the pain I endured. It wasn't all on him. It was me being reckless with my life choices. We had a bond for life, just kids figuring out the wrongs and rights of life.

TAKEAWAY

The choices I made at sixteen and seventeen years old had a profoundly negative impact on my life. However, I have come to realize that a change of environment can be a positive step toward regaining control and finding oneself. In my case, I never considered the consequences of my actions, engaging in unprotected sex with individuals I believed loved and cared for me. Unfortunately, when I became pregnant, I found myself alone and unsupported. It's important to recognize that those teenage boys were also exploring and learning, just like me.

Entering college exposed me to a whole new world of responsibilities without my parents there to guide me. It's not uncommon for many teenagers to lose themselves in the newfound freedom that college offers, often lacking the necessary focus and determination. Remember, every aspect of who you are is important, so take that into consideration when making decisions about your future. Prioritize your well-being and make choices that align with your long-term goals and values.

Chapter 11

SHEEPSKINS AND TIMBS

"RUFFNECK"

Artist: MC Lyte

In the winter of 1990, as I was gearing up for a semester break, still carrying the emotional weight of a recent abortion, an unexpected attraction blossomed. A new neighbor, Lin, had moved into the building right next door to my friend Minnie's apartment. She had a few other girls within my age group living with her. She also had a few guys who would come by to visit her. Among them was Tyreek, and he had a style that caught my eye—a shearling coat and "40 below" Timberland boots.

Minnie told him I was checking him out and introduced us. We got to know each other, and Tyreek was straight up about his life. At twenty-one, he was eagerly awaiting fatherhood, even though he wasn't in a committed relationship with the mother-to-be. His openness impressed me, and I appreciated his honesty.

Despite his reputation as someone not to be messed with in his neighborhood, I was more interested in the person beneath the street persona. I didn't care about his past; I liked him, and the fact that he had a car didn't hurt either. I introduced him to my sister Lee, and we quickly discovered that Tyreek was not just street-smart; he was also the funniest "thug" we'd ever met.

I visited my girl Shawny one day, she had moved to the neighborhood Tyreek was from and now had a baby boy. She expressed concern about me dating Tyreek. He had a reputation. But what she didn't know was that I was no longer the same girl from high school. I had been through some stuff since we last spoke, and Ty came into my life at the right time as far as I was concerned.

He started sharing street wisdom with me, similar to what Keys and Chuck had done before. From the beginning of our relationship, Tyreek made it clear that he didn't want me to argue with men, as he believed they could physically harm me. This was a new perspective for me, as I had always spoken my mind to both men and women. Tyreek insisted that I let him handle any confrontations. Little did he know I had Keys and Detrick to support and protect me.

They met Tyreek after an incident where I disregarded Tyreek's advice and had an argument with one of the guys in my building who worked for Keys. The guy disrespected my sister, and I confronted him. Tyreek walked in while I was heatedly discussing the situation. He sent me upstairs and dealt with it in his own way.

It must have been quite intense, as the guys in the building complained to Keys about it. When Keys and Detrick came to ask me about the incident, Tyreek stepped in, introduced himself, and explained why he confronted the guy. Keys was also upset after hearing how the guy disrespected me and confronted the guy again in front of Tyreek. Their love for me was the beginning of their bond. From that day on, Keys, Tyreek, and Detrick became homeboys. Tyreek would visit me daily, getting along well with the guys in my building and spending time outside, shooting dice with them.

One day, Tyreek came to see me when I was home alone and extremely sick. I was still experiencing pain from the abortion I had in October but was too scared and embarrassed to tell my family. I endured the pain until I couldn't bear it any longer. I finally confessed to Tyreek that I wasn't feeling well, and as soon as my mom returned from work, he informed her. She immediately decided to take me to the emergency room.

Tyreek carried me to my mom's car since I was too weak to walk. I did share with the doctor what I had done. He explained I had an infection and that not completing the prescribed medication or undergoing a faulty procedure could have led to it.

Throughout the entire ordeal, Tyreek stood by my side, taking care of me every step of the way. This was the first time a man had cared for me during my worst moments. He catered to my needs and made sure I had everything necessary to recover. With the medication they provided, I started feeling better within a few days. I felt safe with him and knew he would always take care of me.

It was the day before my eighteenth birthday, and we were all hanging out at Lin's apartment. He said he wanted me to have the best birthday. Later that evening, he told me he had to go out with Lin, his homegirl Nettie, and one of his homeboy Wolfie to take care of something. Lin asked Minnie to watch her kids, and I stayed with her to wait for their return.

They all came back briefly to drop off some cigarettes and stuff, and Ty said they had to go back out once more. It seemed as if their adrenaline was high. Tyreek kissed me and said he would be back before midnight. That never happened. By daybreak, none of them had returned. Minnie and I began to worry. Lin wouldn't leave her children for that long. The phone rang, and it was Lin. She told Minnie they were locked up. Then, Ty called to speak to me. All I remember him saying was, "Boo, I'm sorry. Happy birthday. I'm locked up, but I'm going to make it up to you and explain it later." The phone call was brief; I didn't know what to say. It was all new to me, dealing with someone locked up. He asked me to hold on to his jewelry that he'd left at Lin's apartment. It was some gold rings and a big, gold Gucci link chain. I agreed to take it to my apartment and put it up somewhere safe.

My birthday was miserable. All I wanted was for Tyreek to get released. Everyone but Ty got released the next day. He called every day and started asking me to come see him at BCF Brooklyn Navy Yard Jail. I was thinking to myself, "What do you mean, visit jail? I am a college girl who has never been to jail." He eventually convinced me to come. I told no one I was going. It was the worst place I had ever been. I can still see it: tons of women sitting around for hours to see their men like packed sardines.

After hours of sitting in that hell hole, the officer came to me and said I couldn't see Tyreek because he'd already had a visitor. I was both embarrassed and pissed. I'd sat there all day only to be denied a visit. When he called again, he apologized and explained to me the visit procedures. They were only allowed one visit and whoever got there first could see him. He told me his ex-girlfriend had come. I was hoping she didn't bring a child. I would have never taken my baby into that dirty place. I didn't ask why she was there; I figured she was pregnant and needed to check on him.

I hadn't known that when you decide to have a relationship with a guy living the street life, jail visits were part of the commitment. Taking care of your man when he was down was part of the game. I didn't sign up for that part. It was overwhelming and a culture shock. This relationship was different. I felt like I had a man that was going to love and protect me at all costs. Although he was only three years older than me, he seemed much more mature and experienced than I was.

While Ty was in jail, it was revealed to me that Lin and Nettie were not his biological sisters as they said. They were *like* sisters to him. They were close, like me and Keys. I found out the truth the day his real sisters, Connie and Shareen, came to my house asking for his jewelry. They introduced themselves and said Ty had finally been granted bail. They were going to use his jewelry to get him out.

Tyreek got released, and I just wanted to move forward and leave the past behind with optimism this time. He went on to tell me he'd been arrested for having a gun. I never concerned myself with how the guys I dated made money as long as they didn't ask me to do anything illegal and as long as it didn't define the way they treated me. I just wanted to be loved and respected. How could I judge Tyreek, knowing what I had done to my body twice in one year? At least he was being as honest as he could be with me, even if it was about things I didn't want to hear.

Once he got released, he made me a priority. He started taking me around his family. My connection to his sisters was automatic. Both Connie and Shareen accepted me with open arms. I started hanging out with them and their friends, even when he wasn't around and even though they were older than me. He was the wild baby brother, and I became their baby sister.

I had never been around a group of young women like Tyreek's sisters and family before. They were sweet and would do anything for anyone. He had a large family that were all very protective of each other, and he was extremely protective over them and me. It was all I needed.

TAKEAWAY

Visiting a jail was a world apart from my college life, and it was a wake-up call about the realities of loving someone from a different world. It was a culture shock that challenged my perception of love. Through this experience, I learned that relationships require strength and understanding, even in the face of difficult circumstances. When life takes unexpected turns, it's crucial to navigate them with honesty, open communication, and a willingness to stand by those we care for and to take time to evaluate if you can honestly handle it.

Chapter 12

HOLD HIM DOWN

"IT'S ALRIGHT"

Artist: Chante Moore

Ty and I were going strong until we got into our first argument. I knew he had a daughter, and he eventually told me about another two-year-old daughter he had with the aunt of his older sister's children. I accepted his children and loved the way he loved them. I wanted that for us one day. The conflict came the day I went to his sister Shareen's house, and Ty's oldest daughter's mom, Vette was there, caring for the kids while Shareen was out. She seemed very nice. I had known Shareen's children's dad was Vette's older brother. Ty stepped out for a while, and we stayed at the house talking. She began to talk to me about Tyreek and how they were on and off again.

I sat there with a poker face. I couldn't wait until he got back to ask him about everything. I was not going to deal with baby-mama drama. Once he returned, he saw on my face that I was upset about something and asked me what was wrong. I was not good at hiding my emotions from people I cared about. I told him everything that was said. He was upset and told me it was all a lie. I asked him not to say anything to Vette while I was there because it could become a fight. He told me to wait until Shareen came home and then to ask her what the truth was. She confirmed what he told me.

Tyreek didn't know I had been lied to so much in the past. It was hard to believe the truth at times. I continued to have an attitude with him. We were in the bathroom together, and he was still trying to convince me Vette was lying. After a while of rejecting him, he got frustrated and smacked me in my face. I immediately had a flashback from what Kenji did to me and felt violated. I didn't know how to react. I wasn't sure if he would continue to assault me. So, I just stood there in shock.

He immediately started apologizing, but I checked out, and he saw it. I let myself out of the bathroom and started gathering my belongings to leave. He was trying to talk, but I left. I went straight to Minnie's house and told her what happened.

I was asking myself, do all men cheat? What am I doing to be treated this way? I really didn't expect that from Tyreek. He had been so good to me. He came to my building, and someone must have told him I was with Minnie. He rang her bell, and she opened the door and went into the hallway to talk to him. She came back inside and told me he kept apologizing, saying he should have never put his hands on me and wanted to see me. Minnie and Ty had become close once we started dating, but she didn't agree with what he did.

I agreed to go speak with him. He promised me that it would never happen again and said he would never do anything to hurt me. I told him I wasn't going to be with anyone hitting me, and I let it go. In January, his baby was born, and he brought her to my house to see me and my sister. She was one of the prettiest babies I had ever seen.

It was time to get back to school for the spring semester. I was informed by my school that I would be suspended for the following fall semester due to not taking the MMR vaccine in time. I tried to explain to health affairs about my pregnancy, but the rules were the rules.

I would come from my classes on Wednesday evening and spend the night at Shareen's house in East New York until Monday. She would wake me up to get to school, just as a big sister would do. She wanted me to do well. Tyreek started going to Washington, D.C., where a lot of guys from New York were going to hustle, and he would make sure I had money to commute to school when he came back to Brooklyn.

After being with Ty for a while, I witnessed how he handled people who tried to disrespect him. He could fight really well. He also never went anywhere without his gun. He knew the dangers of the street. He was extremely loyal to his friends, and he loved hard.

He came by one day, and we got into an argument about something stupid. I told him that he never had to come back to see me. He said okay and left. I didn't mean it; I was just not in a good mood. A few days went by, and I hadn't heard from Tyreek. I was feeling sad, but I knew it wasn't that serious. He finally called me, and when he heard my voice, he said, "You're still mad." I said I wasn't, and he apologized, and so did I.

He then told me he had some bad news. I was used to bad news by then. He was locked up again, and this time, on Rikers. I took a deep breath and then asked him how and why. The cops had picked him up on his way back from Delaware for jumping bail on the case he caught on my birthday. He'd gone down with his baby and her mother since he'd wanted his mom to see the baby. I was upset with him being locked up again. He didn't need to jump bail.

Back then, guys would call on the pay phones to talk when they were locked up to avoid us having to pay for collect calls. Ty would call me at the pay phones at certain times of the day. I didn't know what to expect going forward. I didn't want to go visit him after that first experience. This was the dark side of a culture I'd embraced. It wasn't all glitz, glam, and money like the videos portrayed. I had decisions to make. Could I deal with having a boyfriend in jail?

TAKEAWAY

For every action, there is a reaction, good or bad. My actions caused me physical and emotional pain. When things feel fun, free, and dangerous, they are just that! The fun and the freedom disappear once the dangerous behaviors take place. Take time to think about the decisions you make that can cost you everything. I was addicted to the idea of falling in love and was doing anything to get those beautiful butterflies I had once felt back in my stomach. My heart was so pure and ready to love, and after each heartbreak, I kept rolling the dice. Wherever they landed, I laid down for love. Looking back, I had not beaten the odds. I had become a product of my environment. But I didn't think about any of that at eighteen years old.

Chapter 13

I GOT WORK TO DO

"GET IT RIGHT"

Artist: Aretha Franklin

Things at home had changed quickly. My sister was pregnant and was having a baby with Boogie. She made a choice at sixteen, and we were going to stick with her through it. My mom was ready to move away from Herkimer Street. I'm sure raising two teens had been stressful, especially with everything I had put her through. I needed to tell her that I had decided not to return to school after the fall suspension. My mother didn't question my decision. She told me to go across the street to the TAP work center and apply for a job ASAP.

I got hired to work for D'Agostino's, a grocery store. They were upscale for us. I went to training and started working in Park Slope, Brooklyn. We moved to a really nice apartment in a newly constructed two-family house on Jefferson Avenue.

My sister had the baby; it was a boy. I called him "Wah-wah," and he had my whole heart. I would spend most of my paychecks on him. I gave up my space in our bedroom for her and the baby and slept in the living room on a foldable cushion chair, like the ones a lot of college students used. I was never home much anyway, only to change clothes and babysit my nephew.

I loved being a cashier at D'Agostino's. We had to ask customers if they preferred paper or plastic bags. They were conscious of the environment, and they offered delivery options. It wasn't like that on my side of town. I was cool with everyone, but one of my co-workers, Kinard, became one of my closest friends.

My only financial responsibility was giving my mom twenty-five dollars a week. She told us we would never be able to live anywhere for free, so we needed to learn to pay for something. Tyreek and I had a discussion regarding our relationship with him being incarcerated. He told me to go live my life, and whenever he got released, we would see what happened. His only request was for me to take his phone calls. I had no problem with that; he deserved that much from me.

After working at Dag's for a while, I started dating again. There was a cute guy named Marcus with a strong English accent who worked in the stock department. I was checking him out, and he would flirt with me. He was the first Black guy I had ever met from England. I enjoyed the conversations we had about his upbringing. His parents were of West Indian descent, and he moved to America with his siblings in his late teens. He was a hard worker, and I was attracted to that.

I explained my situation with Tyreek. He knew of Ty and his reputation. I told him I'd understand if he feared him and didn't want to date me. He didn't let that stop him. I told Tyreek about Marcus as soon as I decided to give him a shot. Ty accepted it, knowing his situation at the time.

I would hang out almost every weekend after work with my co-workers. Kinard was from Marcy Houses, the place I would go to with Nikay as a child. He introduced me to his friends. They called themselves the UGLY crew, but none of them were actually ugly. They were handsome and fun to be around. I would bring my homegirls to chill with us.

Not long after I started seeing Marcus, my mom got me an interview at her job. They need someone to do Medicaid medical billing, and she suggested it to me. I was interviewed and landed the position. That was a big deal for me. I was going to an office job in Manhattan and making more money, too. With this job, I'd go from $3.35 an hour to $7.50. I was hired part-time with full-time hours, meaning I had no benefits. It didn't matter; I was still covered by my mom's insurance.

One of Shareen's friends started visiting Tyreek. Her name was Gynia. Though I was still taking his phone calls, I was fine with it since I was with Marcus. Gynia was a pretty, brown-skinned girl with a nice figure. She was in the street, and Shareen was looking out for her because she had nowhere to live.

Dating Marcus exposed me to the Caribbean culture. I would party with him at the reggae clubs, and his mother always cooked the best food. He brought me whatever I wanted, even baby formula for my nephew. My family liked him a lot. He even threw me my twentieth birthday party at his family's home. However, we were having issues around the time he gave me the party.

He started to become ridiculously jealous, even with my male friends I met through Kinard. We started arguing a lot about it, and it turned me off. I didn't care about the gifts or anything anymore. He loved me, and I didn't know how to tell him I wanted to break up, so I started staying away more, and I started being unfaithful to him.

TAKEAWAY

Although I was drifting away from Marcus, he didn't deserve me cheating on him. I should have just broken it off. I was anticipating him waiting for his turn to hurt me once the arguing started to be too much. This time, I wasn't going to hang around waiting for it to happen. I was not clear about what I wanted in a relationship at that time.

Being honest with yourself and others can save so many people from being hurt, especially if you care for the person. They don't deserve to be deceived.

Chapter 14

THEM OR ME

"One Woman"
Artist: Jade

Tyreek called one day and asked me to come visit him. He wouldn't let up, although he knew I didn't want to come to Rikers. I finally said I would come on the weekend. I knew he loved me, and it didn't matter who either of us was dating. He would always say he was coming back to claim me. I never took him seriously, knowing he was with Gynia.

On a Sunday, I got dressed and headed to Rikers for the first time. I was praying this experience wasn't as bad as my first one at the jail in Brooklyn. He gave me instructions on how to do everything. I hopped on the G train on Myrtle and Marcy Avenue. By the third stop, I looked up and saw Gynia.

It turned out we were both on our way to see Tyreek. I wondered why he would ask me to come if he had her coming already. Gynia knew I was his ex and that we were still close. She didn't mind, and she said we'd both be able to see him together. I realized it was her weekly routine, and I was the one popping up.

Gynia and I began talking, and she talked about his kids. She mentioned his baby son being at his sister Connie's house. I was confused. He didn't have a son that young because he'd been with me last. Gynia insisted he did and told me to ask his sisters. Ty and I had always talked about babies. I always told him I wanted to have a son since he had daughters already. I then asked if she knew who the baby's mother was. She said yes, his youngest daughter's mother.

I started thinking and getting angry. I remembered Ty telling me that his daughter's mother was expecting again. He'd acted surprised and never mentioned it could be his child. I hadn't cared since it wasn't my business at the time. But it had just become my business.

We finally arrived at Rikers. Ty was in a facility called HDM. Gynia got us registered. It wasn't half as bad as before. They finally brought Tyreek to the visiting floor. He looked so surprised to see the both of us. Gynia was happy to see him. They kissed, and she was talking to him a lot. Me and Ty knew each other well. He was trying to play it cool, but I knew he was uncomfortable.

He kept looking over at me, trying to make small talk and asking about the family and my nephew. He finally said, "So Tina, what's up with you? Why are you so quiet?" Gynia said, "Tyreek, tell Tina you have a son. She doesn't believe me." His attention shifted immediately to me. He said, "What? No, I don't." She was the one who looked confused now. "Yes, you do," she told him.

I started going off on him about lying to me. I was screaming, calling him a liar. I was so hurt. It was like no one else was on the visiting floor but us. We both didn't care that Gynia was there anymore. It didn't matter that we both had moved on. Hearing he had a son had revealed that he cheated on me at some point. I wanted to cry, but I didn't in front of Gynia.

When we finally got to Shareen's house, she knew something was wrong. I told her what happened. Gynia was rushing out to the pay phone to get Ty's call. She came back to the house and told Shareen that Tyreek wanted to speak to her. She went to speak to him and then came back inside. She told me he wanted to speak to me next.

Tyreek kept asking me to listen, and I kept asking him to tell me the truth. I hung up and told Shareen I had to go home. I got on the A train at Euclid and tried to blink back my tears, but they kept falling down my face. I didn't sleep all night.

I went to work the next day exhausted. I hadn't even settled in for the morning when the phone rang at my desk. It was Tyreek. He asked me to let him explain everything, and I did. He told me that the day we got into an argument about Vette and him smacking me, he left feeling like it was over between us.

He'd already had plans to take his daughter to Delaware to see his mother. While there, he slept with his ex. He claimed he didn't know right away about her pregnancy because he got locked up, and he was going to deal with everything when he got released. After that argument, with the way I was acting, I agreed that he could have thought it was over with us.

He said he hadn't wanted me to find out about his son that way. Since we were not together at the present time, I just had to take what he told me for truth. He asked me not to push him away. I still spoke to him on the phone, but I started talking to other guys and becoming more dismissive of everything and everyone.

Near the end of March 1993, Tyreek finally got released from Rikers. I didn't know he was coming home. I happened to be home when he called and asked me what I was doing. I said nothing, and he said he was going to call me back. About twenty minutes later, the doorbell rang. My mother was gone for the weekend. I didn't know who was stopping by.

I went downstairs to answer the door. Tyreek was standing there, smiling. I screamed, asking him what he was doing there. He came upstairs and started telling me about his release. He wanted to see my sister and the baby, but he settled for me since I was the only one at home. I didn't think about anything; I was so happy to see him. He stayed so long that he ended up spending the night with me. Despite our situations, it was like picking up where we left off. I didn't think we were going to get back together. I knew what I had going on, and he had Gynia. We just wanted to be intimate with each other.

Tyreek made it clear that night that he wasn't willing to let me go completely. When he was in jail, he would always say he loved me at the end of every phone call. It felt that way that night.

Tyreek's sisters gave him a party. We called them "just came home" parties. How sad is that? In the hood, when people were released from jail or prison, a party was thrown in their honor as if they had graduated from school or returned from college. I guess it makes sense since everyone always tell their children that the person is away in school. It's how we coped with our Black and brown men being separated from our families. We'd become delusional.

A few weeks had passed since Ty had been home. I had not seen Marcus to officially break up with him, and I had started sleeping with Tyreek again. I knew his sisters wanted us to be together. They felt Gynia's lifestyle was just as wild as his and wanted him to stay out of trouble. Gynia loved him and had a good heart. She wasn't a bad person. Ty and I were just doing what we wanted to whomever we wanted and didn't consider their feelings. I may have had a better upbringing, but I had a lot of baggage with me.

Gynia began to dislike me. She recognized how Ty was when I was around. I didn't know if Tyreek was sleeping with Gynia or anyone else. Some girls he used to date started popping up after he came home. I just kept doing my thing. I had learned how to play the game men had played on me. They loved me, but not enough to be faithful. Finding out about Tyreek's son affected me deeper than I thought. I already had no faith in committed relationships.

Marcus never showed any signs of being unfaithful. Unfortunately, Marcus had become the first victim of my brokenness. I would be up and down with him. Marcus was a good guy. He deserved better than what I was giving him. I was young and inconsiderate of his feelings. I put him in a box with everyone who had hurt me previously. I didn't want him to have the power to do what they had.

It was June 1993. Tyreek had been home for a few months. Although we were sleeping together, we still hadn't decided to get back together. Every year, I hosted bus rides to the amusement parks. That year's trip was to Six Flags Great Adventures in New Jersey, and it was sold out. I always wanted to do something fun to get my peers out of the neighborhood.

The night before the trip, Ty came over and stayed while I prepared everything. He asked if he could come on the trip. I told him no; Marcus had already bought a ticket and was coming even though we hadn't seen each other. He would call and try to talk to me, but I would make excuses not to speak. I felt guilty for what I was doing. Tyreek wasn't happy that he couldn't come but accepted it. Out of nowhere, he told me he wanted us to get back together officially. He said he was still in love with me and wanted me to cut off Marcus. I told him to cut off everyone he was dealing with first, especially Gynia.

The next morning, he offered to drop me off at the bus location. His sisters were going on the trip too. They knew we were messing around but hadn't said anything. I knew I had to face Marcus eventually. Marcus probably thought the trip would be the best time for us to make up. He knew I was always extra bubbly when I was doing something fun with my friends. It wasn't the case that day.

Before I got out of the car, Tyreek told me he was breaking up with Gynia, and he wanted me to break it off with Marcus that day. I told him I didn't think the trip was the place to do it. He told me I'd better do it that day, or he was going to do it for me. I knew what he meant.

Knowing that Tyreek could come to the bus stop after the trip to pick us up and that he was unpredictable, I decided to end things with Marcus on the trip. I told him the truth about how the jealousy and arguing were too much for me. I also told him Tyreek was home, and we both still had feelings for each other. Looking back, this wasn't the best way to end a relationship. Neither of us could leave Six Flags until the bus was ready to head back to New York. That's a long ride after a breakup. That day, I did not ride any roller coasters. But my life became one.

After the breakup with Marcus, I cut all communication with any man who may have liked me. It was all about Tyreek again. But it didn't seem like Tyreek had told Gynia the truth about us yet. He claimed she was only coming around to smoke weed with him and chill with everyone. I knew she would be down for anything he may have been doing in the street while he sheltered me from it all. His gun was the only thing he kept around me. I felt it was to protect us. I watched a lot of girls like Gynia hold it down for their men.

I started adopting some of that behavior from the time I was with Mel, thinking that it was true love. Gynia and I wanted the same man, and I understood her stance. I had nothing to care about but my own happiness, whatever that looked like. I was young with no children and a good job. The only bill I had was for my beeper and the money for my mom.

Tyreek knew I didn't need anything from him, and I knew Gynia had a child and had no place to stay except with his sister. They were those types of people; they wouldn't let anyone stay out on the street. He cared for Gynia, and I knew it. A lot of people I met through Ty, like Gynia, his homegirl Nettie, and a few of my friends, had no other choice but to grow up fast to take care of themselves.

My mom wasn't happy about me getting back with Tyreek. She knew Marcus was a good guy. She told Ty that if she had a choice, it would not be him. Tyreek's feelings were hurt because he respected my mom and loved my family. He would do anything he could for us. He even attended my sisters graduation with us. His family dynamic was totally opposite of mine. His led him to the street early, and mine should have led me away from the street. We both embraced a culture that had no love for anyone.

One night, I was getting dressed to head out to the club with Ty's sisters. We were going to the Sugar Hill nightclub on Nostrand Avenue in Brooklyn. Tyreek asked me not to go and stay with him instead. I didn't want to hear that. I was already prepared to go out. He'd never asked me to not go out before.

I went to the club, and afterward, I headed back to his sister Connie's place to be with him. He wasn't there. I figured he'd found something to do while we were out.

We woke up the next morning, but Tyreek still wasn't there. Shareen asked me to take a cab with her to her place. She seemed aggravated and kept saying no one better be at her apartment. I didn't know why. I had never seen her like that before. I knew his sisters didn't play, even with Tyreek. As tough as he was, they were still his older sisters.

We took the cab to her place in East New York. Shareen knew something wasn't right when we went inside her apartment. She headed straight to the back room and kicked open one of the bedroom doors. Tyreek and Gynia were there, in bed. I sat on the couch in disbelief while Shareen told them to get up and out of her house. Shareen hadn't wanted Gynia with Tyreek, but she'd decided to allow her time to move out and find somewhere to go. Gynia still hadn't left by this time.

I saw what I needed to see in that moment. He looked at me as if he had seen a ghost. I looked at him as if nothing happened. We never said anything to each other. I mean, what could he say? Shareen told Gynia she had to go that day. Tyreek helped her get all her things, and he drove her somewhere. Shareen didn't want to be in the middle of Tyreek's nonsense. I loved her so much for that.

He came back about an hour later and pulled me into the hallway, trying to talk to me. I was mad and told him they were made to be together. They could have a life full of smoking weed and hanging on corners. I tried to hurt him with my words, even though I knew my mouth was dangerous when I was hurting.

Ty said that he'd been upset when I chose the club over him and how Gynia never would have done that to him. I *had* chosen the club over him. But I hadn't driven him to sleep with her. He claimed they didn't have sex, but I didn't believe him. He was trying to have his cake and eat it too.

He had two pretty girls that were in love with him. I knew him well enough to know that he felt he owed her since she had been loyal to him. I was just too naive to pick up on it. He told me that when he dropped her off, he officially broke up with her. He promised me it was over, and I believed him. I wanted to give him some grace. After all, I wasn't innocent. I had hurt and cheated on Marcus. My ego wanted to believe that Ty only wanted me. I was being immature and wanted to show Gynia that he'd always wanted me. I told him if it happened again, we were done.

I decided to go home and change. I went back to hang out at Shareen's with everyone and spent the night there with Tyreek. Early the next morning there was a knock on the door. It was Gynia again. Someone let her into the apartment. It could have been one of the kids. She knocked on the bedroom door where Ty and I were sleeping. He asked who it was, and she asked if she could talk to him for a minute.

He jumped up and told me to let him see what was going on. I knew she was a fighter and was hurt. Although I knew he would never let anything happen, I didn't want her to catch the drop on me while I was lying down, so I got up when he went outside the bedroom.

Of course, I was trying to hear everything. I could hear her crying and pleading with him. I heard her say she loved him and was there for him when I wasn't. He responded, "I love Tina! Do you want me to be with you knowing I'm in love with somebody else?" My heart felt bad for her, but the selfish twenty-year-old was glad he told her he loved me. I was thinking, why should I care about her feelings when no one ever cared about mine?

She ended up leaving, and he came back into the bedroom. He asked me if I was happy after hearing him tell her the truth. I told him yes and let's work on us. Tyreek and I had broken up with two people who loved us and had filled the void while we'd been separated due to his incarceration. We hurt people for our own selfishness. We should have told them both from the beginning of the possibility of us getting back together.

TAKEAWAY

Be sure that when you make decisions in your relationships, you do it with care and compassion. Extend the same courtesy and grace you want from others. Treat people the way you want to be treated. I had opportunities to do the right thing, but I chose my own happiness at the cost of someone else being hurt. That selfish behavior doesn't end up well for anyone. It begins to poison relationships.

Chapter 15

DANGEROUSLY IN LOVE

"I CAN'T TELL YOU WHY"

Artist: Brownstone

Ty and I were back in love and going strong. He would always say we were going to get married and have a bunch of babies.

He was again traveling back and forth to Delaware, to his mother's house. His mother, Diane, and I got along, and sometimes, I would go down on the bus after work on Fridays to see him. She would sometimes come to New York for a few days to visit too.

It was July, and "hot" was an understatement. I was hanging out at Connie's house after work, and Ty's mother had come up. Connie didn't feel well, and neither did I. I was cramping a lot with horrible back pains. We decided to walk around the corner to the emergency room at St. Mary's Hospital.

We both got evaluated. The doctor came to me and told me there was nothing wrong with me—I was pregnant. I couldn't believe it. I was so happy. We left the hospital, and I told his sister and our friends. Everyone was happy. I knew we wanted a baby together. I told Diane when I got back to the apartment, and she was also excited for me.

Tyreek was in Delaware, and I had to wait until he called to tell him. He finally called, and when I told him, he thought I was joking. Once I said I wasn't, he was happy about the news. I didn't care about his lifestyle. I was going to have my baby with the man I loved. I had his family's support, and my heart was filled with joy.

However, I would quickly find out that my feelings about the pregnancy would be different on the other side of town with my family. Tyreek promised to be back for my first prenatal visit. I started getting morning sickness and unbearable headaches. It was difficult getting through my workdays, and I hadn't told my mother yet. I had to hide how sick I was becoming. My partner at work, Drew, was the only one I told. We were close, and I trusted him. He knew everything about me and Tyreek.

I was home one day, sitting in the living room, when out of nowhere, my mother came to me and said, "I know you're not laying up in my house pregnant." I said, "Yes, I am." Her response was, "Well, go stay with the person who got you pregnant." She said my sister told her. She called my dad to tell him, and he came over to have a quick conversation. The only thing he said to me was, "You know you're going to be raising that baby by yourself." Then he left. My mom had told him about Tyreek's criminal background.

My feelings were hurt, but I did as she said. I packed my stuff, gave my nephew a kiss, and left. I was twenty years old and working. I didn't expect that response from my parents. Why didn't I get the same grace as my sister did when she got pregnant? Maybe it was because my mom liked Boogie and not Tyreek. It didn't really matter. I was used to handling my business and emotions on my own. I went to Shareen's house and told her what happened. She said I could stay in her son's bedroom since he never slept in there. I was grateful I had somewhere to go, especially with Tyreek still in Delaware.

My mom did love Tyreek's sisters, but she just wanted him to get his life together. She had recently got Shareen a job working with us as a medical biller, and having Shareen working with me was the best. She took care of me at work and at home. Tyreek always stayed with his sisters whenever he was in New York. Once Ty got out of jail, he didn't want to live in New York, so he spent most of his time in Delaware at his mom's where he had a room. I wasn't ready to pick up and leave New York. Once I became pregnant, he had to come back to New York for me.

Shareen and Mason, her children's dad, made me as comfortable as possible. Mason made sure I ate a balanced meal every day when I came home from work. I appreciated the love they extended to me when I needed it the most. I did what I could for them to show my appreciation. It didn't matter how I was feeling emotionally or physically, I just wanted my baby to feel my love. It was the first time in my life I wasn't calling my mom's apartment "home." I was forced to leave unprepared.

I went to work every day like everything was fine. I made it to work late one morning after having the worst morning sickness on the train and had a verbal altercation with my new team leader Jacque. She pointed her fingers in my face, and with all my built-up anger, I threatened to break them. She reported me to the staff manager. He was close to my mom, so I figured he would be fair. But it seemed as if he sided with Jacqué. He was about to reprimand me when I told him that I was pregnant and had an episode of horrible morning sickness. Kellis was also a manager. She witnessed everything and vouched for me. We were close; she was Christian like Drew and also talked to me about God. I needed it more than ever. My office manager calmed me down, gave me a hug, and congratulated me.

That day, I decided to share my news with the entire office. Everyone seemed excited for me, even Jacque. She called me into her office and apologized. My mom no longer had to feel ashamed or deal with her bosses after finding out she had another daughter, unmarried and pregnant. A few days after the incident at work, my mom drove over to Shareen's place to see me and told me I could come home. She felt bad putting me out. I refused. I was being stubborn and felt the damage had been done already.

I was making a mental stockpile of all the things that had been done to me. My parents hurt me when they didn't support my decision, and I had a lot of unspoken anger building inside of me. I had to focus on having a healthy baby and finding out where we were going to live before I gave birth. I was having a baby with a lot of uncertainty.

I knew my mom was going to love my baby. She had already started driving across town to bring me any food I was craving. After a few weeks, Tyreek finally returned from Delaware. He was upset with my mom after what she had done to me. I didn't hate my parents for wanting a better life for me. It was how they expressed it to me that I didn't like. I was young and in love. They were concerned parents. It was a harsh reality for them that I had grown up and was making my own life choices.

My morning sickness was unbearable. I was four months pregnant when it finally stopped. Those pregnancy headaches were worse than the ones I had after my incident with the cops. Ty stayed in New York for a while. I tried never to miss work while I was pregnant. I was part-time and wasn't getting paid for sick days, and I refused to let anyone's opinion about my pregnancy slow me down. In trying to do it all, I even fell a few times and fainted on the train one day. Thank God my mom was with me.

My mom was trying her hardest to make amends. She picked me up every Saturday to shop and hang out. But I still had something to prove. I took all my disappointments so far in life to go hard for my baby. I had a reason to be strong and keep doing what I needed to do.

At a little over four months pregnant, I still didn't have a baby bump. I wasn't picking up baby weight due to the morning sickness. I had become a high-risk pregnancy from losing weight instead of gaining. I was glad Tyreek was there with me. I didn't sleep well if he wasn't.

My grandmother was visiting from Detroit, and I had planned to go see her after work. Tyreek was hanging in front of the building, joking with some girls all night. I woke up tired, and I had an attitude with him, so I decided not to go to work. I only wanted to see my grandmother. Only me, Ty, and Mason were home.

I told Ty why I was mad at him and that I didn't want him to come with me to my mother's to meet my grandmother. We started arguing because he knew I was being mean intentionally. He was mad and said that he should have stayed with Gynia. My temper went up. I threw my sneakers at him. I said, "I should have stayed with Marcus." We started tussling. He was holding me down to stop me from throwing things at him. At the same time, he reached for his gun in the drawer. I started screaming and calling Mason. He ran into the room, yelling at Tyreek to chill, and took the gun from him.

While he was calming Tyreek down, I was able to pack up most of the things I had there. He tried to stop me, but I was mad and scared after he tried to pull the gun on me. That was the first time I saw him emotional. He cried and begged me not to leave. Nothing he said changed my mind at that moment. I called a cab and went to my mother's house.

I made it to my mother's place with all my belongings. Once I saw my nanny, I felt a little better. I smiled and masked all my pain again. My nanny knew something was going on. She was easy to talk to and always gave me great advice. I just couldn't speak what my heart felt at that time; the words wouldn't come out. So, I closed myself in the bathroom and silently cried. I never told my mom or grandmother the real reason I came home with my bags. I told my mother I needed to stay with her while I looked for a place. I enjoyed the time I had with my grandmother even though I was missing Ty.

Whenever I was around, he would be brief with me and only ask about the pregnancy. One day at Connie's, I decided to let go of my pride and asked him if he still loved me. He said he did, but I hurt him that day I left. He said he was tired of me walking away whenever I wanted. I kind of understood him; I never went hard for him like I did with Mel. If he had chosen Gynia before I got pregnant, I would have just moved on. We managed to forgive each other and move forward. Being pregnant made me want to fight harder for our relationship.

I continued to stay with my mom while looking for a place of my own. I also continued to let my attitude get the best of me. I didn't realize how jealous and insecure I had become while being with Tyreek. Any interaction he had with a female upset me.

Once, he was playfighting and joking around with his oldest daughter's mom, Vette. She was family; this was nothing out of the ordinary. After she left, he was ironing my work clothes for me. He was talking to me, and I was being really short with my answers. He asked me what was wrong, and I told him. He said I had an effed-up attitude, and he was tired of dealing with it. I told him he didn't have too anymore.

He was so mad; he'd done nothing wrong, but once again, I was leaving.

I called my bestie Nikay from Connie's phone and asked her if I could come stay the night. I grabbed up all my things and left the apartment. He started yelling downstairs, "Tina, you serious? Stop playing and come back upstairs; it's late." I kept walking. He came behind me, trying to talk, but I wouldn't hear him.

He drew his gun and told me to come back with him upstairs. Out of fear, I turned and walked back toward Connie's building. This was another incident where my actions caused his reactions to be extreme. It had become our norm. Argue, make love, and move on. He was his most vulnerable with me, and I was so distant with him emotionally. He was always explaining himself whenever I felt insecure about anything concerning us. It was who I had become after all the things I had been through. We had started seeing the worst sides of each other.

I used my words as a weapon against Tyreek, and violence was the only way he knew how to react to conflict. I had fought boys in my childhood and men who disrespected me on the street prior to meeting him. Tyreek was different. I'm not sure if he knew it or not, but that's where my fear of him really began. After the two incidents with the gun, I felt that he would hurt me and my family if he got angry enough.

I ended up apologizing that night for my attitude. I remained dangerously in love. I wanted to be the one to love Tyreek enough for him to change his life around and have a family.

We decided to get a place together before the baby was born. I was tired of sleeping in my mother's living room and at his sister's. I needed a place to call my own. We eventually found a place in Bed-Stuy on Hancock Street. My mom brought some things for us. I would still stay with her when Ty went to Delaware since I was scared to stay alone.

Tyreek was back to spending a lot of time in Delaware. He made sure he didn't stay away longer than two weeks at a time. I was six months pregnant when I went down to bring in the 1994 New Year with him. I'd finally gotten a baby bump, and I wanted his mom to see me. She couldn't stop kissing and rubbing my belly. Ty and I had some minor disagreements at times but were doing a lot better for a while.

During my seventh month of pregnancy, things became worse than ever between Tyreek and me. Things started falling apart after Boogie told Tyreek a lie about me.

Boogie had told Ty that Mel was still coming around and that I wanted to be with him. It was the biggest lie ever told about me. I didn't know how Ty could believe any of it. It turned out Boogie was upset with me after I told my sister I heard he'd cheated on her. I never expected him to get revenge this way. He was like a brother.

Tyreek came home, flipping on me, saying he didn't know if the baby was his. I barely saw Mel, and Ty knew I got pregnant three months after he came home from jail and that I spent most of my time with his family. But he didn't believe me. This was the turning point in our relationship. It was one thing after another from then on.

He called one day while he was in Delaware and started questioning me about this guy I cheated on Marcus with. I was afraid to answer him because his anger was becoming rage toward me. At first, I denied knowing the guy. After we hung up the phone, I called him back and told him everything. The guy's name was Melvin. He was nothing to brag about, just a typical, cocky hustling clown. He was annoying, so I'd cut him off. But clearly, he'd been talking about dating me to other guys on the block.

Ty didn't care that I had called him right back with the truth. He kept asking why I lied. I didn't want Tyreek to do anything that would send him back to jail. I knew his temper when it came to me and his family. I also knew whatever he heard must have embarrassed him.

I was no longer looking like Ty's big-mouthed but cute little college girlfriend. I began to look like a mean and deceptive, lying young woman. I happened to see Melvin before Ty caught up with him. I cursed him out like he'd stolen my baby from my belly. He took something from me: Tyreek's trust. He'd lied about being with me recently to boost his ego when he'd known it had been almost two years. He tried to apologize for anything he'd said jokingly, but I told him the damage had been done. I was pregnant with Tyreek's baby, and I told Melvin to never speak to me again. I'm sure Ty also told him the same thing. I didn't see him hanging around my mother's neighborhood again, and if he did, he avoided me at all costs.

TAKEAWAY

Blessings come at the most unexpected times, even if you feel unworthy of them. Being pregnant was my blessing, a chance to embrace love and to grow up. This time around, I was going to stand in my truth and have my baby no matter what happened.

You may be uncomfortable with some of the things that come along with your decisions. Don't play the blame game for your choices. Own them and continue to be strong in faith. Trust yourself. I made the choice to do what I needed to do for myself and my unborn child. I moved out because I knew I was going to keep my baby no matter how anyone felt.

Sometimes, in life, you just don't know how to act or what to say. I didn't know how to express my feelings of insecurity. I was becoming a mom with unresolved issues within. We are better people when we can articulate what we feel. Not being able to express what you feel can lead to internal turmoil. There are so many resources now that we didn't have back then. I wish I'd had a professional to help me and Ty learn how to effectively communicate before things got worse.

All the lies dismantled any chances of our relationship getting better. A relationship of any kind without trust won't last. We didn't trust each other anymore. I knew the love was fading due to mutual disrespect. Lies never care about who tells them.

Chapter 16

FAIRY HELL

"IT HURTS LIKE HELL"
WAITNG TO EXHALE SOUNDTRACK
Artist: Aretha Franklin

Ty had lost all respect for me and began speaking to me disrespectfully. He would bring up things he heard about me dating during the time he was locked up as if he didn't know I was talking to other guys. I was seven months pregnant; those feelings should have been expressed when he came to me as soon as he was released.

I had become severely depressed. I was only there for the baby. To get a reaction out of me, Tyreek kept saying maybe it wasn't his baby. I was about to have a baby with someone who was acting like he hated me, and I started to regret being with him.

Cheating on Marcus came back to haunt me during the most important time of my life. The only joy I had was that the baby was coming. I began to drown myself in my music. I would get home from work, and if Tyreek wasn't there, I would put my headphones on my belly to let my baby hear the music that brought me comfort. If he was home, I would do whatever I needed to do to keep the peace.

The verbal abuse and threats had become constant. I wanted to avoid things getting physical while I was in the final month of my pregnancy, so I stopped using my weapon, which was my mouth. I had to pretend to be happy, knowing the man who had once protected me had become the one I needed protection from. The only thing I'd done right this time was to keep my baby. My white picket fence fairytale love had become fairy hell.

My co-workers gave me a beautiful baby shower on my last day of work before I left on maternity leave. Tyreek came and brought me a dozen long-stem roses. That day was a good one for us. After that, I was home every day, and we were making it work.

I was almost two weeks overdue when I started having labor pains. I was with Minnie at the repass on Herkimer Street. I got in touch with my mother and Tyreek. Minnie told him to meet us at the hospital.

My doctor had already planned to induce me the next day anyway, so they admitted me. Minnie and Tyreek walked me up and down stairs for hours, but no baby. Minnie finally left. I was so hungry, and they didn't allow me to eat anything.

Ty was right by my side all night, holding my hand and rubbing my back. He was acting like the Tyreek I first fell in love with. The next morning, I still hadn't dilated much. The midwife told me they were going to have to induce my labor. My mom arrived and gave Tyreek a break so he could run home to change his clothes. He made it back right on time. My mom was holding my hand to push when he walked through the door. She moved out of the way and stood against the wall, watching as her second grandchild was born.

Ty coached me and cheered me on. The baby was out in three pushes. It was the most painful but beautiful experience I had ever had. We'd done it. We'd held it together long enough to bring our baby into the world. My whole world changed on April 29, 1994, at 12:14 in the afternoon. Tyreek kissed me and said, "You got your girl." He knew I'd wanted a boy at first, but then switched it up once I started shopping and saw all the cute girl clothes.

I was happy my mom and Ty were able to share that moment. We already had a name for her: Eboni. Ty had always wanted a little girl with that name, and it fit her perfectly. We gave her both of our mothers' names as her middle name. She was perfect to me. Tyreek was so excited after the delivery that he left me in the delivery room to follow the nurses with the baby. He said he was making sure nobody tried to take her because she was so pretty. My dad and brother came to see me at the hospital the day she was born. My parents always showed up when it mattered the most.

The first week home it was all about her. Tyreek was the dad I knew he was going to be. She looked so much like him and his family, and Ty kept saying she was his twin. Shareen gave her the nickname "Nu-Nu" after she saw her for the first time.

I had made a choice to breastfeed her after reading up on how beneficial it was for babies. But I was having a hard time adjusting. I didn't have a breast pump when I first got home, and my breasts were filling up too fast. I was producing more milk than the baby needed. I was in so much pain. My mom told me to put hot towels on my breast and take a hot shower to allow the milk to flow. It worked to relieve the pain until she brought me a breast pump.

I also didn't have an appetite to nourish my own body. I'd become weak from losing blood and being anemic. Slowly, I gained an appetite, and it got better.

Me and Tyreek developed a system: I would take her in the morning while he got some sleep. He washed all her clothes out by hand and hung them up every week.

I began to get better physically but not emotionally. I had severe post-partum. No one even noticed, not even me. I didn't know what I was feeling. I was disconnected from everything, and I was allowing Tyreek to do everything for the baby. Even if I wanted to, he barely let me at times. We would go out, and he would hand me the baby bag, and he would carry the baby. I hated that, but to avoid an argument, I never said anything.

After a couple of weeks, he started back with disrespect if I said anything that annoyed him. Any time my mom would come by or buy something for me or the baby, it triggered him. Somedays, I was threatened or belittled. The next day, there were flowers, cards, and I love you.

He would not allow my mother to watch the baby. She would try to give us a break, and he would make me tell her to bring the baby back. He said if she didn't like him, she didn't like his baby. I know it was to hurt her feelings. It put me in an awful position. My mom would ask why, and I would just beg her to bring the baby back. She would. I guess she knew it was him, not me.

I knew Tyreek had to deal with a lot being with me, but so did I by being with him. He felt he could never do enough for us to impress my parents. He started taking out their rejection on me. I was isolated from everyone, even his family, at times. I had lost my voice; he controlled everything.

I hadn't realized how noticeable my depression was until my cousin Ken came down from Detroit for the baby shower that my family had planned for me. She'd had her son a year prior. A few days before the shower, I was at my mom's house, and she looked at me and asked what was going on. I was confused. She said, "Look at what you're wearing." I still have the picture of the outfit. It was a flowery shirt with some yellow linen shorts. It was probably the ugliest thing in my closet. My hair was pulled back with no style to it. She said, "You're always dressed, so fly, this is not you."

Ken knew me well; we told each other everything. I just couldn't bring myself to tell her what I was going through. I didn't want another one of my family members to dislike Ty. Ken had picked up immediately on what people around me every day didn't see. No one talked about depression or postpartum depression. I felt torn down.

The baby shower was at my Aunt Jo's daycare center on Albany Avenue and Eastern Parkway in Brooklyn. Only two of his family members made it there on time before it was over. It felt like my family was rushing into the shower. I was not feeling like myself at all. It was a horrible day for me. I only remember who was there from the pictures I have. That entire day was a blur—except for when Ty came to me while I was sitting down and whispered in my ear that Boogie had brought Mel with him. Fear took over. I was so scared; I had butterflies in my stomach.

No one else was afraid. They had never been on the other side of Tyreek's wrath. This could have been a death sentence for everybody. Boogie brought Mel inside, and he congratulated me. All I could do was say thank you and hold my head down. I don't think Mel had a clue what he was involved in. He truly only came to support.

Tyreek told Mel to never come around us again. I don't know what would have happened if Boogie wasn't my nephew's dad. Ty felt disrespected, like everyone was trying to come between our relationship, and he didn't know what to believe anymore.

My family became public enemy number one to him, including me, after that day. A few days after the shower, Ty called my mom's house to address the situation. He and my sister started arguing. Once Tyreek hung up, he was so angry he turned and punched me in the stomach.

It was so hard that all I could do was fall to the bed and try to breathe. I had just given birth two weeks prior. He saw the pain he'd caused and fell onto the bed next to me with another "I'm sorry." I just started crying. I knew that level of physical abuse could possibly escalate. The punch was the defining moment for me.

He had gone too far, and there weren't enough "I love you's," "I'm sorry's" or cards in the world to keep me around after that. I just needed to figure out when and how I was going to leave him. I didn't know how to tell his family or mine that he was hitting me. No one knew. He was mindful of how he handled me around his family.

Finally, his sisters saw him hit me. That's when I knew I was making the right decision to leave. His cousin had passed away, and his sister warned me not to say anything to him when he showed up late to leave for her funeral. I didn't listen and asked him where he'd been. He smacked me in front of everyone.

I couldn't believe that he'd gotten so comfortable with putting his hands on me that he did it in front of his family. I needed to speed up my exit plan. After he smacked me, I made a joke about it, saying my eyes told my mouth, "Why did you say anything?" I laughed about it with his sisters, but I got a revelation that day: If I stayed any longer, I would become a person who normalized that behavior. There was nothing funny about being humiliated and physically assaulted in public. My misery began to show at my workplace. Kellis and Drew covered me spiritually. If it wasn't for them, I would not have leaned on my faith as much as I did to get the strength to leave.

Kellis would give me scriptures to read daily, and Drew kept the gospel music playing all day at work. I would be home alone with the baby, reading scriptures and playing gospel music. My mom knew things had gotten bad after my baby shower. She picked me up one day and took me to see a spiritual woman, Ms. Mabeline. She was a friend of my dad's sister, Aunt Jo.

I didn't know anything about her. My mom told me Ms. Mabeline prayed over me as a baby when I used to cry in my sleep all night, and then the nightmares stopped. I went to the place and sat with her. She remembered me as a baby. She told me everything I was dealing with, things my mom didn't know. The most hurtful part was when she said, "He's abusing you. You have to leave him. If you stay, he will end up killing you by accident or on purpose." She went on to say, "If you leave him, he will never touch you again. You will be okay." Then she added, "Your baby is going to be very gifted and smart."

Ms. Mabeline gave me a Bible scripture to pray daily; it was Psalms 91, a prayer of protection. Anytime fear came over me, I read it. I had to clean up my own mess. It was truly a thin line between love and hate. I had become only an object of desire. I hated it when he touched me, but I had to keep the peace. Our hearts were no longer in love.

Yes, his heart was broken from the things we went through. But it didn't warrant verbal or physical abuse. I could no longer live a life with guns under my mattress, not seeing my friends, and scared to be alone with a man I'd once wanted to be with forever. I felt imprisoned, though without handcuffs or cell gates. Music and prayer kept the little bit of sanity I had left. I was mad at myself for allowing him to take away my voice out of fear. I hated that I had no control over anything anymore. Not even the baby I carried for almost ten months. I was just existing, not living. He felt my energy, and it made him resent me more. I missed my life and my smile. I felt ugly and empty inside and out.

He was going back and forth to Delaware again. I stayed home alone with the baby. One night, I lay there, me and my Nu-Nu. I didn't really know her. I don't know if she knew me for anything other than feeding her my breast. I fell asleep and woke up feeling like something was holding me down, not allowing me to reach my baby. I started praying and felt a release. I grabbed my baby, held her in my arms, and just cried. I told her I loved her and I would protect her, always, because she didn't deserve a life like this. I also asked God to forgive me. I asked him to help me get out of my situation.

After, I prayed and cried. It was like all the postpartum was gone. I was in survival mode as a mother. No therapist. Just me, God, and my baby. I felt like myself again. I needed to belong. This baby was mine and here to stay. Ty and I both loved her dearly. We just couldn't be together. I wasn't willing to die for it anymore. I had died emotionally. I wasn't going to physically. No more guns being drawn on me. No more being called a bitch and a ho. No more punches, smacks, or kicks. I chose to live for me and my baby.

This was Tyreek's grand finale of handling me his way: He called me while he was in Delaware. He started telling me that he met a woman, a nurse, and she knew how to appreciate him. I knew he wanted a reaction. I gave him one: I told him to be with her.

Ready or not, Tina was back! I called my mom that next morning and told her I was taking the day off to move out. She told me she would come to help me get my things. I called Shareen and asked if she could come help me because I had to move out of that place. She didn't know I was leaving her brother. I told her I was going to stay at my mother's, and Ty couldn't stay until I found another place. I gave her all his belongings. I only needed mine and the baby's things.

By the time I got the last bag out and we dropped off Shareen, Tyreek was calling my mother's house. He had driven back to New York. He knew he'd gone too far the night before on the phone, and my not responding to his calls alarmed him. He went to our place to find nothing and no one there to abuse anymore.

He was on the phone, threatening me and telling me to bring the baby to his sister Connie's house. All he wanted was his daughter. I wasn't going for that trap. If I went, I would have been back in harm's way. He kept calling, and though I tried to keep my mom out of it, he said if he had to come get the baby, he was going to hurt my family.

My mother heard him. She called my Aunt Jo, who lived down the street, but she wasn't home. I called my dad and told him what happened and to get to New York fast. He said okay. My dad and his sister, Aunt Jo, reminded me of Tyreek and his sister Connie. They were no joke. My mom would tell me stories about how violent they were back in the day.

Tyreek came to my mother's block with two of his friends. He was screaming my name and to bring the baby down. My mother was scared of what he would do. So, she decided to take the baby to him to protect me and stop him from making a scene. That didn't work. He began to verbally disrespect her after she handed him the baby.

My sister was visiting my family in Detroit at the time, but my nephew stayed home with my mom. My mother returned upstairs and called the police. She was so scared he was going to hurt us that she grabbed my nephew, went inside her bedroom, and locked the door.

Ty then called the house phone again and told me to come downstairs to get the baby. She was only three months old, and I was still breastfeeding. Maybe he realized he couldn't leave with her. This time, I said okay. A peace came over me. All the fear, anxiousness, and timidness had left my body. I went downstairs to get my daughter.

He acted as if he was going to hand her over to me in the doorway, but instead, he began to fight me while still holding my baby. I protected myself the best I could. All I remember was trying to guard my face while kicking him to protect myself. I didn't know what he was going to do. I was in survival mode and didn't realize he had the baby in his arms the whole time.

My mother's landlord heard the commotion and came out. She pulled him off me and said she was calling the police. He finally stopped. I grabbed my baby and ran up the stairs. He hopped in the car with his friends and left. A lot of neighbors were outside, seeing everything.

The cops and the ambulance arrived around the same time. I was bleeding over my left eye, and the baby kept crying. My mother finally came out of her room. I called Ty's family and told them what he had done and that if he came back, he was going to get arrested. I didn't want him arrested; I just wanted him to stay away from me.

The ambulance and the cops took care of me. A scar from the gash over my eye is a reminder of that day. The EMTs were trying to cheer me up by saying even with a swollen eye, I was still pretty. It made me smile and took some of the embarrassment away.

My dad arrived at the hospital with Aunt Jo. He looked at my face, and he never said a word. He turned around and left. I was told later that he drove around Brooklyn looking for Tyreek. I was glad he never found him; it would not have been good for any of us.

I finally understood what my dad meant the day he said to me, "You're going to be raising that baby by yourself; watch and see." It hurt me to accept that I was becoming a single mother at the age of twenty-one. Once I was released from the hospital, my parents had me pack up some things. They didn't think it was safe for me to stay in Brooklyn. My dad took me and the baby to his place. The next day, he booked us a flight to Detroit to stay with my grandmother.

I had no real relationship role models in my life. I had experienced the ugly side of break ups. Love cut me deep and pierced my heart in places that couldn't be stitched up.

TAKEAWAY

In the same way, I glorified the hood culture, I also glorified the fairy tales, movies, and music about relationships. Fairy tales are fabricated stories with magical happy endings. Me and my sister loved watching teen coming-of-age movies, especially the ones that actress Molly Ringwald starred in, like *Pretty in Pink* and *For Keeps*. Though the cast was all white, they had the same issues we dealt with during our teen years. My fairy tales had become horror stories.

When you are faced with a decision that not only affects your well-being but also someone else's who you're responsible for, choose wisely. Some choices are harder to make than others, especially when your heart is involved. The heart wants what it wants. Your mind will guide you to do what's necessary even when your heart wants to be comfortable with what it knows feels good at times. Trust yourself enough to have the strength it takes to deny the things that can cause a lifetime of damage in order to live a healthier life, no matter what it is you have to walk away from.

Chapter 17

FREE TO BE ME

"DREAM ON DREAMER"

Artist: The Brand New Heavies

Who would have thought I would be living in Detroit? I had left everything behind for my freedom and peace. My nanny would come and get the baby to give me moments to myself. She'd ask me if I wanted to talk about anything, and I would always say, "No, I'm okay." I just needed to think about how I was going to provide for this baby with no income.

I would wake up and use the boom box radio my nanny had to play one of the cassette tapes I brought with me. I needed my music, just like a smoker needs cigarettes. I kept playing a gospel song, "How can I say thank you" by Hezekiah Walker. I knew those prayers had come through for me. I had a chance to begin putting the pieces of my life back together.

I couldn't cry about what had happened and didn't have many words. I was glad my family was right there for me. They could have said I was stupid for staying or even having a baby with a man who didn't have plans for the future. My grandmother and cousin Kendra made it all right for me as soon as I touched the soil of Detroit, Michigan.

Ken knew how to cheer me up! She knew I loved to party in the "D" and that I hadn't danced the night away in a long time. I needed to go out and enjoy myself. Shoutout to Ken's friends who became my girls:

Betty, Tressa, Malika (S.I.P), Michelle, Monique, Wendy, and Tonia. They always showed me love whenever I was in town. I partied with them the same way I did with my girls in New York.

My nanny would just look at me and smirk. I knew she was thinking, "You are going to be just fine." After about two weeks in Detroit, my dad called and told me he was sending a plane ticket for me to come home. He told me that I needed to come home and return to work to be able to take care of my daughter. I had a good job there, and there were more opportunities in New York.

I'm sure my dad didn't want Ty to feel like he had control over me. My dad assured me that I would be protected. I packed up our stuff and did as he instructed. I returned home and settled in at my mom's place. After about a week, I called Tyreek to speak with him. I was in mama bear mode to talk only about the baby.

We agreed to meet at Shareen's place. I knew she missed the baby and wanted to see her. I arrived, but I never went inside. He came out and was loving on the baby. Shareen took the baby while we talked. He cried while expressing himself about all that had happened.

I knew it wasn't a sympathy cry to make me take him back. This was a remorseful cry. He apologized for everything. I felt his pain, but I couldn't show any emotions. I knew what had to happen going forward.

New beginnings were scary but necessary. My life depended on them. I had devalued my beliefs before Tyreek even met me. I had already become disconnected from reality. Our relationship was toxic from the time we got back together after his release from Rikers. His distrust and my fear were an ever-exploding bomb. Our love couldn't recover after the physical abuse. I didn't want him to "love me to death" literally anymore. Broken people, breaking each other was what we had become.

I gave him two choices. I told him we could be the best co-parents, or we would remove ourselves from his life if that wasn't what he wanted. He agreed to co-parent and love her unconditionally. The only thing he asked of me was for me not to be with anyone who would have guns and drugs around our daughter. If I didn't want it with him, I shouldn't allow it from anybody. I understood what he meant. Even with everything we went through, he still loved me and would lay down his life for his family. That included me.

We both agreed that no matter what, we would always be family. From that day, we kept our word to each other. It was rocking at first, trying to accept our new norm. I did curse him out a few times if he dated someone that I knew. But we would laugh about it and move on. We became better friends and co-parents than we were lovers. The best love we both had to give was to our daughter.

I had to return to Detroit a few weeks after I came home. My grandmother (Nanny) got married to her boyfriend, whom we lovingly called "Pop." She had been with him since I was in Junior High School. Me, my sister and cousins were her bridesmaids. I was still breastfeeding at the time and had to stop because I had a fever on our way home traveling back to New York. My daughter was four months old. It was great to witness my grandmother remarry in her sixties after my granddad was murdered when my mom was only two years old. She did give me a little piece of hope that forever love can find you at any age, although it hadn't found me yet.

TAKEAWAY

It was not easy to accept the fact that I was going to be a single mom. I wanted to have all my children with a man that I loved. At twenty-one years old with a three-month-old baby, I had no idea what life would be like going forward. I just knew I had to make a change that would be the best for all of us, and it was. I will forever have a love for Tyreek because we created a child together while being in love. But I knew that we had to go on living separate lives while doing the one thing in life we had to do together: raising our daughter.

Making changes for the better is not just for you but for those that are a part of your life. You may have to be the one to take the initiative to do what others won't.

Chapter 18

NEW BEGINNINGS, BAD CHOICES

"Let It Flow"

Artist: Toni Braxton

I had found a one-bedroom apartment in Brownsville after staying with my mom briefly. The rent was $550 a month. I furnished it with my income tax return and gifts I received from my house-warming party. Though I had my freedom, I had a lot of financial responsibilities.

My older sister Charlene would ship me Huggies Supreme diapers from where she lived in Houston every three months. That saved me a lot of money. I never asked for any financial help from Tyreek, my parents, or anyone I dated. My mom always helped, even if we didn't ask. I didn't want anything that would make anybody think they had control over me ever again.

Both of our families were a great help as I got myself back together. Especially Tyreek's family. Shareen and his cousin Donya were my go-to sitters for everything. I knew Nu-Nu was in good and safe hands. My Aunt Jo allowed her to come to her daycare center until she was of age to go to regular daycare.

I was able to return to my job as a medical biller. I even got a little promotion. The director took a liking to me; she recognized my hard work and had me moved to work directly with her team full-time. I needed the pay raise and benefits.

Some days were harder than others. My daughter was sick a lot after she turned one. She had asthma. There were days when I was at the emergency room all night with her and had to get up for work with little to no sleep. My mom would try to be there with me. Tyreek wasn't in New York most of the time. I never bothered him much for anything unless I needed him to come take her to give me a break.

My sister and I both had been through a lot and became single mothers. She eventually moved out of my mother's place and got an apartment for her and my nephew when she was nineteen years old.

That September, my dad got married to his long-time girlfriend, Barbara. I wore the same dress from my grandmother's wedding. My sister and I showed no happiness for him that day. We were in our feelings. My mom wasn't invited, and we thought that was disrespectful because we had always been inclusive with his wife during holidays. I think I was just angry with everything and everyone due to my own failed relationship and hurt.

Even though I started going back out and dating, I was never the same girl. There were times I wanted to love, and other times I ran away from it. I used to love the idea of love. I think both Tyreek and I jumped back into dating, thinking we could erase what happened between us.

I had never had a break between relationships. I had become a relationship rebounder. Looking back, I had a pattern: out with one and in with the next.

I would break it off with a guy with no remorse or regrets if something they did or said turned me off. Sometimes, it was only a sexual attraction for me. I thought at the time I had it all together. But I didn't. Love hurt me, while lust had no expectations of me.

Most of the time, I labeled those lustful encounters as relationships. As I reflect on my life, the pattern of rebounding started after my relationship with Mel.

The cheating and rejection may have unknowingly affected my self-esteem. It also made me a honeymoon stage hopeless romantic for a while. I wanted to feel those butterflies again. I was like a drug addict trying to get that high again. It was not happening.

During that period of letting go of Ty and embracing my womanhood, there were a few times I tried to let my guard down and love again wholeheartedly. There was never a happy ending with any of them. I can't blame it all on the men.

I had become a young woman with a not-so-nice side. I could say things that cut deep if I was upset. After getting my voice back, I used a lot of profanity and was very defensive and dismissive, all from unaddressed anger and needing a defense mechanism. After dealing with so many traumatic experiences—molestation, police brutality, heartbreak, physical abuse—I told myself I'd die defending myself before allowing anyone to ever violate me again, and I still mean it. Not all situations required my aggressiveness and rude responses.

My time alone listening to music allowed me to tap into my emotions. That was my only therapy. I could sing along when I was in pain and dance in my happiness. I buried the trauma deep and became guarded, like most who have suffered in silence. My body and heart had been damaged and scarred long before any heartaches and breakups. Anyone can judge a lifestyle without knowing what caused their behaviors.

I knew I was being judged. Some people looked at me like a party girl. Some as a girl that dated drug dealers and street hustlers. As long as they didn't call me a bad mother, I didn't care. Nothing came before her well-being. I made sure our home was our sanctuary, our place of peace.

We stayed at that apartment for maybe a year before I moved. My mom brought home applications for my sister and me to fill out for new subsidized apartment units. My mom knew we could not afford market rent while raising children. We both got approved. Thanks, Mommy!

The newly renovated apartments were in Bedford-Stuyvesant. I was glad I was moving back to my side of town. All three of us lived within walking distance from one another. I met Patty, who had a son, Taury, and lived in the apartment above me. We developed a friendship at once. She became my big sis, best friend, confidant, and everything within a few months. We could not be any closer even to this day.

As young as I was, I never allowed my friends to make my apartment a hangout spot. It was me and my baby's safe place. They would come over periodically, but they knew the rules. I never allowed smoking in my apartment. I didn't smoke weed or cigarettes. If I had company, my daughter would not be home, or I would ask Patty to watch her while I entertained my guest. I respected the other tenants, and being the youngest one at the time, I didn't want any complaints.

The rebound relationship I was attempting to have ended when I moved into my apartment, and he asked for keys. That was when I realized I wasn't ready to live with anyone and broke it off with him. It was a major trigger for me. I needed time to myself.

I should have known I needed even more time to process my life when a guy I'd been dating for a few months named Teddy got locked up on Rikers, he was also from Marcy Houses, and I started visiting him there. We weren't in a relationship at all, only sleeping together. To this day, I don't know what his charges were. I don't think I even cared. The story didn't change. It was just a different character. Rikers Island became the home away from home for the guys in my neighborhood who had no guidance or father figures.

For me, it started to look like for every freshman class going into college, there was a freshman class headed to jail. There weren't many alternatives offered to inner city youth of color who committed lower-level crimes. They definitely didn't have the resources or funds for paid attorneys or proper legal representation. They were sent to C-74 on Rikers Island, Spofford Youth Detention or received harsh prison sentences. This is when I began to see that the scales were unbalanced.

The majority of visitors were women of color with their children. Going through the process to visit was not pleasant. The commute, searches, and wait time alone were sacrifices to support their loved ones. I often thought to myself, "Where are all the friends to these guys? Why do I only see baby mamas, mothers, sisters, and wives?"

Most of the visitors were like a tribe, supporting each other. It was an unspoken language that was understood by those of us making that sacrifice. When I first began going on visits, I had the nerve to try to make myself believe I was better than the women I saw at every visit because I was coming from my nine-to-five job with my suit and expensive shoes on.

I was no different. I even met one of my closest friends, Kay, from visiting Teddy. I eventually broke it off with him and stopped visiting once I found out he had someone else visiting him on days I was at work. She had just given birth to a child. That was all I needed to hear. He pleaded to be with me. But once again, it's the same game with different players. I moved on with my life. After he was released, he tried to rekindle things. I respectfully declined and kept it moving. I should have never invested that much time with him from the start. Again, I was looking for love in all the wrong people. I vowed from then on to break off any relationship with men if they expected me to become a "jail wife."

TAKEAWAY

Celebrate your new beginnings! Take time to pat yourself on the back for doing something right. We beat ourselves up for the mistakes we make. I celebrated getting my own apartment, my promotion, and not staying in a relationship just to have one. I was maturing slowly. We all evolve in time. Never count anyone out because their process is different than yours. I was doing okay for what I'd been through.

Co-parenting is only hard if the parents choose to make it hard. We chose to remove our feelings regarding our relationship in order to ensure our daughter felt loved and supported by both of us.

Chapter 19

DISTANCE BETWEEN US

"WHERE'S THE GOOD IN GOODBYE"

Artist: The Braxtons

I decided to take a trip to Detroit with my daughter in 1996. We traveled by Greyhound bus. I didn't like flying much, and this was cheaper. It was a thirteen-hour bus ride. I loved that it gave me time to put my music in my ears and shut out all the noise of my world.

Once I arrived and settled in, me and Ken did what we normally do: hit the club. One night, we ran into Riz's cousin, Mark. He managed to reconnect Riz and me. I hadn't seen him in almost five years. I couldn't believe Mark remembered me, but he did.

Riz lived in the same place. He came around every day I was there. It was like nothing had changed from the summer we met. We picked up where we left off. Once we reconnected, I would travel to see him and my family every few months.

Riz and I started having conversations about permanently living together and how that would work for us. In the middle of 1996, we decided since I was already established in New York, he would move in with me. He didn't want the street life anymore and wanted to find a better way to provide for the four children he had with his ex. I knew how much he loved them. I told him to make sure their mother knew she could call any time they needed him.

He figured New York would be a fresh start, and Riz moving to New York was what I needed at the time. I needed to see if I could live with someone I loved or if it was the long distance that was making me comfortable. I took a trip by myself over the weekend to travel back with him. I knew he'd made a sacrifice for me and wanted him to be comfortable traveling to my big city for the first time.

The entire bus ride, we both kept laughing, saying, "We are really doing this." He settled in well. We spent the holidays like my one happy family. It was a new world for him to experience. We never had arguments and talked out any disagreements. We laughed more than anything. Having girls himself, he helped me a lot with my daughter.

Tyreek was caught up in Virginia in a legal situation again. I didn't make it my business. Whenever he was around, he made time to see his daughter, and that's all that mattered to me. I was happy, in love again, and it was good.

After a few months, Riz started to miss his children a lot. I don't think he expected how difficult it would be not seeing them all the time. He also hadn't found work and didn't like the fast pace of the city. I knew how much he loved me, but as a parent, I would never let anything keep me from my daughter. So, I understood when he told me he needed to be closer to his children.

My heart was shattered. He knew it and tried to keep reassuring me it would always be us. I bought him a one-way ticket back to Detroit when I got paid. I figured the sooner, the better for me mentally. I stayed strong watching him get on that bus, although it felt as if I couldn't breathe. I didn't want my two-year-old to see my tears, but they kept coming down on the train ride back from the 42nd Street bus station.

We tried the long-distance relationship again for a little while, but it was too emotional for me every time I had to leave. I tried to move on. I stopped communicating or asking Ken if he had come by the house. I listened to The Braxtons' song, "Where's the Good in Goodbye," and my SWV New Beginnings album on repeat. I had twenty-four-hour cry sessions. It was my thing—cry enough to release the pain and recover.

TAKEAWAY

Sometimes, letting go of what you love hurts deeply—relationships never just affect those who are in them. Riz needed to be back with his children, and they needed their dad. I am very sensitive when it comes to children. His leaving devastated me. Loving him hurt because I couldn't have it forever. *Love, don't love nobody!* That's how I felt after ending things with Riz. It was a hard blow to my heart. I told myself that there was no such thing as true and forever love. I was internally angry with men and just wanted to protect my heart as much as possible. I was numb to love for a while. I didn't want it.

Chapter 20

A PARTY AIN'T A PARTY! UG BABY!

"A PARTY AIN'T A PARTY"

Artist: Queen Pen

I managed to pull myself together and get back to life as I had once known it. I spent a lot of time hanging out in the Marcy housing projects with my homeboys. I would put my daughter in that little blue McClaren umbrella stroller, and we would hit the street. I decided to get back to hosting my bus trips to amusement parks. I was back to selling out buses to have fun with friends.

My boy Chris approached me about throwing a party with him and Kinard. I told him I was down. It was always me and a girl we called Queen hanging with Kinard, Chris, Big Ray, Roddy, Milk, Dollar, Kek, Spank, Spider, and Tee. Ray's little sister, Nik Nice, would tag along too.

We planned the first party in 1996 at the YWCA in Brooklyn. Big Ray didn't want to be a part of thc group at first, but he sold a lot of tickets for us. He was able to get rappers Jay-Z and Sauce Money to come out. They were also from Marcy housing projects. It was early in Jay-Z's career. We got a lot of support. It was all love!

I sold all my tickets and made money. I had all my girls come out along with my co-workers. It was like old times again with Tyreek's sisters and their friends Bee, Renee, and Naima (RIP). We would go to the legendary Jones Beach Greek Fest or the local clubs in Brooklyn: Sugar Hill, the ARK, Africa House, or the Brothers in Business Parties at the South Oxford Tennis Club and dance the night away.

The night of my party, they all came to support me, along with my besties Nikay, Tash, and my sister Lee, to name a few.

The success from the first party gave us the momentum to do another, bigger and better. We were no longer just going to the party; we became the party. The new kids on the block of Brooklyn party promoters! ME AND MY BROTHERS! WHAT UP BROOKLYN! It was a takeover. I don't think any of us could have imagined becoming one of the hottest promoter groups in NYC. Big Ray came on board after the party at the YWCA. It was the birth of Ugly Productions. The fellas already had the Ugly crew; they came up with that name. But this time, it was business. Money was involved, and only a few of them became official party promoters.

Shortly after our first party, I started PGP—Pretty Girls Promotion—an all-female independent street team. Back then, record companies had their own street team promoters at the hottest nightclubs and events to promote their artists. I decided, "Why not have my own independent street team?"

Being independent gave me the freedom to work with various record labels and choose what I wanted to promote. It was natural for me to think outside the box to create or develop things. I recruited a few of my friends who enjoyed partying and my sister, of course. I also had a few girls we met at places like the Greek Weekend in Philly.

Ugly Productions blew up so fast. Everyone knew who we were. We started having parties more often and getting better venues in Manhattan. I eventually dissolved PGP and focused on Ugly Productions.

I didn't have the time to do both. I was working full-time and being a mom, and although things were going well, I was making more money by promoting parties than by being a street team promoter.

We had people from all over New York attending our parties and wanted the best locations for safety and travel. We started out with one rule: no jeans or hoodies. You had to dress up. People wore the best to our parties—mink coats, Versace, Fendi, Prada, and Coogi sweaters. Men were wearing Gators shoes. The ladies were wearing their designer bodycon dresses, catsuits, and outfits they had made by local seamstresses.

I had my go-to designer Hot CoCo; all I had to do was tell her my vision, and she would make it happen. She never missed the mark. We recruited promoters from throughout the city after a while. The fellas had two female groups that came on board: 2000 Inc. and the Honeyz. We also started collaborating with other known promoters down the line. But the ladies were a great addition for me since I was the only female promoter in our group.

It was not that easy for me being a mom and female party promoter. I had to be out promoting from Thursday through Sunday during the times we had an upcoming event. It required more than just partying; it cost money to make money, just like operating any business. I had to pay for a sitter at times for my daughter. It wasn't just a fresh haircut and good cologne like the guys. I had to look good – hair, nails and outfits. I often had to set boundaries with men, so they understood it was business.

We didn't have social media then; it was all word of mouth. I understood my position as the only female in the group. I had to bring the pretty girls to party and sell tickets to guys who were going to spend money at the bar. I never worried about anyone disrespecting me at our parties or while I was out promoting an event. The guys were right there.

We also started booking worldwide DJs, like DJ Mister Cee and DJ SNS to name a few. They had people dancing out of their clothes, they were partying so hard. We never had an incident of violence, even though we had a mixed crowd of street guys, entertainers, and the working class. We showed people a good time. A few people met their life partners at some of our parties.

"A party, ain't a party if Ugly didn't come through it!" was our motto. We supported other promoters that supported us. Shout out to Party Mix, Brothers In Business, Brooklyn Mecca Dons, Score Entertainment, and Gator Productions.

One year we all traveled to support Party Mix when they hosted a trip from New York to Virginia Beach. That's what made Ugly Production stand out. We knew how to get a party started and always showed up with good energy, ready to cater to our people. If I met someone who could bring value to our team or a guy who liked me, I made sure I had them show up for us. I pulled my weight, and we would use everything we could to give our supporters a great time.

The fellas started hosting skiing trips. That was a big money maker for promoters. I decided not to invest in the trips, but I still played my part and sold tickets for them. I didn't have the time or money to take that on. The ski trips were an addition to the business and unforgettable.

I continued to host parties and met a lot of people in the entertainment business. I was even considering changing careers to work for a major record label. I wanted to work in either artist development or marketing because I loved to do them both. Party promotion was not a career move. It was exciting in the beginning; I could hang out with people's favorite artists and celebrities. But I had a lot to consider being a single mom.

TAKEAWAY

Getting back to hosting trips and promoting parties was what I loved doing at that time of my life. I didn't want to focus on being in a relationship. I was a young woman living and learning along the way. I didn't do everything right. I knew I had my own personal issues. I never took bad energy with me anywhere. I dealt with my stuff behind closed doors. Business is business, I had to represent the brand—UG BABY!

When you decide to do business, you cannot allow your personal issues to affect your commitment and professionalism.

Chapter 21

LOYALTY TO THE END

"CREAM"

Artist: Wu Tang Clan

After Riz had left, and during the years of promoting parties, I had no relationship goals. Anything I had going on was only about a good time.

I decided to go to a basement party in Bed-Stuy with the fellas one night. There was this tall guy there that everyone kept talking to. He asked Big Ray to introduce me to him. He was very flashy. He was well-dressed and had on lots of jewelry like the drug dealers in the late '80s. I asked Ray the rundown and found out I was right. His name was Neek, another one for Marcy houses. I peeped; he was a player who loved the ladies. I wanted nothing to do with him. But Neek wouldn't let up.

He approached me nicely, and that's what made me have a conversation with him. He was about seven years older than me. We exchanged numbers that evening. He kept it real from the start. I knew he was a hustler. He had no children, but we had a few things in common: We loved to dance, dress, and party. He also made it no secret that he loved jewelry and women. I had no problems with any of it. I still didn't want a relationship with anyone. Neek was like a big kid full of energy and fun.

We began seeing each other. I felt I could tell him the truth about anything. I told him about Teddy, and he didn't care. I told him I couldn't commit to loving anyone, and after my previous relationship with Riz I didn't think I could have love like that again. His response was, "Just give me a chance."

He did everything he could to love us. He would tell me he admired how I worked hard and took care of my daughter by myself. He said he would always make sure we were good. That was our bond. If my daughter was sick, he showed up at the hospital or my apartment, no matter how late it was or how tired he was from partying or hustling. He was loyal.

When someone tried to tell him about me and Teddys past relationship, he checked the guy and told him he knew already. I was grateful Neek understood me. That's the type of relationship we had. It was no rules. I didn't have to explain what I had been through to him. He just got it. It didn't matter if he was seeing other women; he was my friend more than anything else.

The crazy thing for me was how men could date as many women as they wanted, have children with multiple women, and were rarely ever judged by their peers for their behavior. But women who decide to live their lives out loud, not sneaking or hiding, but just living as they learn, especially young women, are crucified by the very men who wish they had an opportunity to be with them.

My daughter's third birthday had come. I wasn't trying to let anyone deep into my personal life, but Neek had made it clear that he wanted to be there. Tyreek was coming and it would be the first time he was going to see me with someone else. I never brought anyone I was dating around, I had that level of respect for him.

They both had reputations in the street, and I knew there was no fear from either of them. It made me a bit nervous, but I knew they would respect each other. That day went well with no guns drawn, thank God.

The reality was that I was damaged and could not completely open my heart to Neek. He was out there enjoying his life as well. He eventually was locked up for a crime and had to do some time. He was my homie, and I wanted to see what was happening with him. He had become more like a best friend.

I was clear from the start with Neek that I could not do jail time with him. He told me there was another woman willing to do the prison time with him. I told him to let her, and he moved forward with her. He wasn't willing to change his lifestyle for me. As much as I cared for him, and though my loyalty ran deep, I didn't want to raise my daughter in that environment.

Instead, I wrote letters to him whenever I had time and answered his phone calls. I kept the vow I made to myself to never become a "jail wife." We had a lot of love for one another. Yes, I loved him, but I wasn't in love with him. We had a hood, street code type of love.

He eventually came home, but things had changed drastically for me. We remained friends. He was just truly a solid man. The realist. His sister Naj is one of my closest friends. Neek later got married to a woman he met a few years after his release. Not long after he came home from another prison bid, he was killed in a motorcycle accident.

I saw him the week before his accident. He was telling me he had a baby on the way. He was so excited to see my daughter. He gave her some advice and told me to give him a call. That would be our last conversation. It's been about twelve years now. I know he would have been an amazing dad. Rest in peace, Neek, the homie for life. A good man gone too soon.

TAKEAWAY

There will be times in the midst of your brokenness when God will send signs through people to remind you that you're never alone. These types of people come into your life with no expectations other than to make sure you know you matter. When the time comes that they are no longer here with you, find a way to always celebrate your memories of them. Neek was that for me as a young, single mom. I will forever be Tina Wina, as he used to call me.

Chapter 22

AM I THE OTHER WOMAN?

"MARRIED MAN"

Artist: Kelly Price

The summer of 1997 in New York was a good one. I was doing my thing, and I met so many people from being out on the scene. I was going on dates, but most of the summer was busy with promoting our upcoming parties.

I was hanging out with my cousin Mena one day at the grand opening of her friend's barbershop called Brooklyn's Finest. She introduced me to a guy named Damien. He reminded me of Sean "P Diddy" Combs, just heavier. She told me he was a Correction Officer and had his own record company. I had dated a Police Officer before and knew they could be players just like the street guys. I was twenty-three at the time.

He offered to drop me home after the event. He was driving a Mercedes-Benz. I liked the fact that he had a good job, not selling drugs; and driving a nice car didn't hurt. He was in his early thirties, just like Neek. I was always attracted to older guys. I felt they were more mature than guys my age. I learned that wasn't true. After talking to Damien for a few hours, he seemed cool. I was relieved when he said he was single. I told him I had just started dating again after Neek had gotten sentenced. We exchanged numbers, and I went upstairs.

He called me the next day and asked to take me on a date. Since we both loved music, I had him take me to the Tower Records store on

42nd Street. They had a movie theater in the basement. It was a dope spot, and I figured he'd really like it. I was right.

He offered to take me out to eat, but I was tired, so I told him I was good with Burger King. He thought I was joking. Clearly, he wasn't used to a woman turning down dinner. I was always myself, I could be classy, and a bit hood, all in one.

Some guys liked it, and some didn't. I never faked being who I was for anyone. I knew, at times, my energy could be a bit much to handle. Damien seemed to like it all. We had great chemistry. He would ask my opinion about his artist and the music he was producing. It was refreshing for me to be with someone who understood and loved the entertainment business.

I started to let down my guard and decided to go in with an open heart. I didn't want to have any reservations. I felt he could be the perfect person to have a future with, finally.

I took a trip to Detroit after meeting Damien. I talked with Riz and told him why I had cut off all communication. I explained to him I had found someone who wasn't living a street life and wanted to have a relationship with him. It hurt Riz, but I knew we needed closure.

I continued to keep in touch with Neek through letters and calls, no matter who I dated. I told him everything, even if he didn't want to hear it. Damien was going to be the one I didn't have to worry about going to jail—he worked there. I let myself embrace my feelings after I felt I could love him.

We spent a lot of time together for about four months straight. Around that December, I started feeling like I was more invested in the relationship than he was. He started to become a no-show. If

I needed a ride to pick up my daughter from daycare, he seemed to never be available. I knew he worked overnight and did a lot of overtime, but those things hadn't stopped him from spending time with me before.

His lack of concern started getting to me. I would call and leave derogatory messages, going off on him. I figured he had started seeing someone else. I even began to question my demeanor, thinking maybe my rough exterior and nonchalant attitude had turned him off. I began to have feelings of rejection.

He managed to show up to take me out for my twenty-fourth birthday. Assuming he was an all-around good man since he had a career and treated me so well in the beginning, I still had hope for us. As I said before, older guys knew just what to say and do to get what they wanted.

I wanted to believe in us so badly to avoid another letdown in a relationship that I stopped trying to figure out what was going on. I continued to let him pop up whenever he chose to make time for me. I had fallen deep and hadn't realized it. I also didn't want to be with anyone else at the time; my life was busy enough.

It was around April 1998 when my cousin Mena came by to see me with a male friend. After they left, she called and told me the guy she was with had asked about me, and she told him I was with Damien. The guy, whose name I don't remember, said, "How is she with him when he has a wife and a newborn baby?"

Mena said she couldn't believe it. The guy went on telling her that he had helped Damien move out of the place he shared with this woman. He even described what the woman looked like. There I was again, hearing news about a baby. It felt like I was living in a movie on repeat. I hadn't spoken to Damien for a while because of his disappearing acts. I wanted to get the truth from him directly.

After hanging up with Mena, I sat at my dining room table, mad at myself and in shock. All this time, I'd been hard on myself while this dude could have been playing me. I paged him, and he called me right back. I made casual talk and then pretended to miss him. I knew he would come right over, mainly for his own pleasure, and he did.

Damien got to my apartment about thirty minutes later. We sat on my couch. I caught him off guard and asked about everything. He denied it and said whoever told me that was a clown and how people hate and have their stories mixed up. He never said what part was mixed up.

That was a red flag for me. I felt like he was the one lying. I just had no proof of anything, and it did come from a guy who'd been checking me out. I knew if Damien was lying, the truth would reveal itself eventually.

What Damien didn't know was that I had made up my mind—until I got the truth, I was going to start dating other people again. Those feelings I had about us having a future together disappeared after that day. I was going to continue to see him and anyone else I wanted going forward.

TAKEAWAY

I found myself desperately trying to recapture the love I once felt. Unfortunately, my efforts were in vain, and each time, I ended up getting hurt even more. It dawned on me that I wanted Damien to reciprocate the same love and openness that I had shown him, but it seemed that wasn't his intention with me. When someone is hiding something, they can never fully invest themselves in a relationship because their focus is on concealing their truths.

Don't lose yourself in the pursuit of someone who cannot give you the love and openness you deserve. True love should bring out the best in both partners, with honesty and vulnerability at its core.

Chapter 23

LUST AND NO LOVE IN THE CITY

"AIN'T IT FUN"

Artist: Paramore

Damien was the icing on the cake. As far as I was concerned, no man deserved my love, or me, ever again. I had my mind made up that it was the last time my heart was going to make decisions for my life. I walked into many relationships open to love. Damien blindsided me. I should have known better. I had never dated someone that could possibly have a wife. He had even taken me out for Valentine's Day, although he would disappear at times. I figured a man with a wife would never do that. I introduced him to my family and went out in public places with him. All my friends knew we were together. Where was this wife?

Having mixed emotions about him, I tried to limit the times I made myself available for him. Going forward, he would just get in where he fit in.

I started hanging out more often, especially on Wednesday nights. I would hang out at a restaurant named 3B's for comedy night. It was hosted by one of New York's legendary hosts, Ray Dejon, and one of New York's Kings of Comedy, the comedian Talent.

Me and my homegirl Niqua and I would go every week. It was the place to be in Brooklyn whether you liked comedy or not. The baddest chicks, hustlers, tough guys, and promoters would be there.

Niqua was fly and knew a lot of people. She was a hairstylist and would do my hair for all of my parties at her salon, Doll House, located in the basement of her brownstone. She was the only person I trusted to do my hair. She would pick me up or I would take a cab to meet her on Wednesday nights.

I decided to stay home one Wednesday. Niqua went to 3B's and then called me up after, telling me about a guy who had approached her asking about me. She told me he was dressed nicely and had on some expensive jewelry. Niqua said he was with a bunch of guys who also had expensive watches, jewelry, and they all were good looking. We laughed, and I told her I would definitely be there with her the following week.

They were the type of guys we were attracted to that caught our attention. "Money, power, respect is the key to life," just as Rapper Lil' Kim said in her lyrics. It was the cultural mindset of young women like us back then.

We showed up the next week looking good and ready to laugh and chill. Niqua pointed the guy out to me. He was with a bunch of guys who all looked like they had money. I noticed his outfit. He was dressed in the latest fashion brand back then, "Ice Berg", and had on a diamond-encrusted Rolex aka "Rollie". He was on the short side, around 5 foot 5, but that didn't matter to me.

We were seated at our usual table. The waiter came over and said someone offered to buy us drinks. She pointed at the guy Niqua had shown me. He sent a bottle of Moet Champagne and Hennessy. I would drink socially.

I don't know why I drank— it was never necessary. I always had a natural high from energy. I've only been intoxicated three times in my life. Those hangovers were enough for me.

The guy eventually made a gesture for me to come over to where he was standing. I walked over to him and formally introduced myself and thanked him for the drinks. He told me his name was Clayton, but everyone called him "Cee". We exchanged pager numbers.

Clayton and I didn't speak right away after we met. That Friday, I went out with one of my homegirls, Wanita, to a party hosted by one of the biggest promoters in the city. We ended up partying at the same table of some guys I saw often at parties. One of them was a short, stocky, dark-skinned guy. He introduced himself as Hersey and kept offering me drinks. I kept telling him I was good. He eventually told me that he had been watching me for a while at parties and 3B's and had wanted to meet me. We had such a good time with them, we exchanged numbers.

The next day, Hersey called and asked if he could take me out for dinner and a movie. I told him sure. I called my friend Wanita to talk about the party. She said to me, "Did you get Scoot's number?" I told her no; I had met Hersey. She said, "That's not the guy's name you were talking to. His name is Scoot."

I got so nervous. I told her he was on his way to pick me up, and he'd given me a fake name. Scoot was a guy who had a reputation in Brooklyn, just like Tyreek. More people knew of him and his crew for getting money and being dangerous.

One thing Tyreek asked of me after our breakup was not to date anyone he knew from the street. He didn't want things to get ugly if someone did anything to me or our daughter. Scoot was one of the people he'd mentioned.

Even though I knew I had been lied to, I still decided to go on a date with Hersey, aka "Scoot." He arrived in a burgundy 740 BMW. We went to a movie and a restaurant in Manhattan. While in the movie theater, I called him Scoot to let him know I knew he'd lied about his name. He laughed and said, "You got me." At the restaurant, he explained why he gave me a fake name. He'd realized I didn't know who he was, and if he had said "Scoot," I may have rejected him due to his reputation. He was right.

The date was nice. He was a complete gentleman. He asked me at the table how he did do, and I told him very well. He took me home, and I allowed him upstairs since my daughter wasn't home. We sat and talked until daybreak. I explained to him why I couldn't date him and that I had a child with Tyreek and what we agreed upon.

I asked Scoot if he knew Clayton and told him I met him at 3B's. He told me Clayton was a good guy and would treat me well. He knew it couldn't be him. About a week later, he was arrested by the Feds. He called and let me know.

I was no stranger to phone calls or letters from jails and prisons. Mostly from Johan, Neek, and Tyreek whenever he would get jammed up. Scoot had become one of the homies and was added to the list. Back then, I probably had more jail mail than bills. Even my biological brother was locked up in New Jersey for a short amount of time.

I ran into Clayton again at 3B's. He told me he'd tried to reach me, and I decided to give him a shot after my conversation with Scoot.

Clayton paged me the next day as I was headed home from work. We spoke briefly and decided to meet up later in the evening.

Patty agreed to watch my daughter for me. He pulled up and called me, and I went downstairs to him, he was driving black Lincoln Navigato. I wanted to have a deeper conversation with him. I was twenty-five, he was thirty-two. He was single with two children, but he got along well with their mother. I was relieved to hear he had no baby mama drama.

He asked me if I was hungry and said he hadn't eaten anything. Earlier on the phone, he'd asked what kind of food I liked. I told him seafood, steak, and pasta. He told me he had somewhere we could get food that late in the evening. He made a phone call, and I heard him say, "I'm on my way."

We shot across the Williamsburg Bridge, into the city. He pulled up in front of a restaurant called Vincent's in the Little Italy section of Manhattan. I had never eaten at any of the restaurants on Mott Street. He went inside and came back out with a menu and with a white guy. The guy waved at me. I waved back in shock. I'd never dated a guy who even had white friends.

He told me that it was the manager. They were closing, but they kept the kitchen open for us. I was blown away. This was some stuff I had only seen on television. What was Clayton's line of work that he could have restaurants stay open for him?

During our conversation that evening, I asked him what he did for a living. I figured he could only give me one of two answers: in the entertainment industry or a drug dealer. He told me he was in the music industry. Just like I thought. But he was different from Damien. He seemed to be more in business with people from the music industry, while Damien was more hands on with the actual talent and production.

Cee started calling me every day. During that time, I landed a new job at Columbia Presbyterian Hospital as a receptionist for the Department of Oral Surgery. My daily commute was much longer now that I was traveling from Brooklyn to Spanish Harlem. I had been referred by one of the managers who left my old job to work at Columbia. She wanted to take me with her. I was honored she thought of me that highly. She ended up getting me a job there, although not with her.

After almost two weeks of going out and talking on the phone, I finally allowed Clayton to come upstairs to my apartment. We just sat and talked for hours. He asked me about my Mother's Day plans since it was a week away. I told him I had none and that I had a trip planned to Cancun in a couple of weeks. He asked if I received gifts from Tyreek on Mother's Day. I told him no and that I didn't expect anything since we weren't in a relationship. He said he always gave the mother of his children a gift even though they weren't together and mothers should be celebrated. I said that was thoughtful, but I was good. I wasn't ever going to tell him what I went through with Tyreek and why I didn't need gifts from him, only respect.

Thursday before Mother's Day, he called me at work. He was shopping with a friend at Jacob the Jeweler, a well-known jeweler to entertainers. He told me to make sure I had a sitter; he was picking me up that evening to take me out.

He picked me up and had a few of his friends going out with us. We ended up in the city, at the All-Star Café, located in the heart of Time Square. Clayton wasn't pleased with the food at the restaurant. I was fine with it. He paid the bill for everyone, and we left. He apologized to me about dinner, and as we drove off, he asked me if I had to go home right away. I didn't; my daughter was with a family member. He made a call to someone and told me he wanted to make up for the bad dinner. He had a bottle of Dom Perignon champagne on ice in the truck, but I told him I didn't want any.

While driving, he presented me with two boxes. He told me which one he wanted me to open first. I quickly picked up on a few of his personality traits: He was very cocky, but a giver. I opened the first box. It was a thick Cuban link gold chain with a diamond pendant. He said, "Happy Mother's Day," then told me to open the other box. It was the matching bracelet to the chain.

I was speechless. I didn't want to become emotional in front of him, but no one I had ever dated had bought me gifts that expensive. I had never been romanced on that level. We had not been intimate. He just valued time with me and showed it in his own way.

We pulled up to one of the more expensive hotels in Queens near the airport. A gentleman greeted us at the concierge desk. I started getting negative thoughts. Maybe this was his norm. He must have seen my facial expression because he told me the guy was his homeboy and was the manager.

When we entered the room, all I could smell was food. He'd had the concierge order it from a popular restaurant in Long Island. The room had so much food: fried and steamed shrimp, bread, pasta, and beverages. All my favorites. He was so thoughtful.

I'd been so blown away by the way he treated me since we met, I decided to stay over with him there. I hadn't felt appreciated and special in a long time. He made sure I was home in enough time to prepare for work.

I told Clayton about Damien and why I wasn't dealing with him as much anymore. He didn't care. He just wanted me with him mostly all of the time. He always said he had never dated anyone like me, so straight up and funny. He knew his money didn't impress me. The situation with Damien hadn't been settled, and as much as Clayton was doing for me, I didn't want to get too close.

I was living life like every day was my last and just wanted to enjoy it. Thinking like that made it easier for me to do what I wanted unapologetically. Clayton offered me any and everything. We ate at the finest restaurants. If an artist had a show and he knew them, all I had to say was that I wanted to go. He made sure I was treated well. He had great relationships with a lot of business owners throughout the city. He introduced me to a different lifestyle that I enjoyed.

My first time eating at a Mr. Chow restaurant on 57th Street was in 1998 with him. He had me go with him to a meeting he had one night with rapper Busta Rhymes's manager. Clayton being connected to people in the industry had me considering applying for a job at a major record label again. I love music that much. I would be at studio sessions with him while famous artists were recording their music. At times, I would have to tell him to take me home. He would give my friends money just to drive me to meet him or if they went shopping with me.

After a while, I felt I was just complimenting his arm. I figured all those nice gestures were nothing for a man who had money. Eventually, he would get bored and be on to the next chick, and I didn't want to get attached to him. I continued dating other people even after he said I was his girl. I just didn't trust him or anyone at the time.

I had planned a trip to Cancun, Mexico, for Memorial Day weekend. It was me, Big Ray, Milk, and my girl Naj Neek's sister. Clayton asked me if I needed anything. I told him no although I was tight on money and was grieving the loss of my dad's mother, my Grams. I only told Scoot about her dying when he called. He had two of his friends come and take me and Niqua out to a restaurant called "One fish two fish" to cheer me up. He was locked up, but always checked in.

I don't know why I was becoming so paranoid with Clayton, so early in our relationship. It was another too good to be true thing for me, everything he did was over the top. I guess. I felt he was lining me up to control me with his money. I still had major triggers. The more he tried to do for me, the more I pushed him away.

A lot of people went to Cancun for spring break from the States, and Brooklyn was deep. We partied from the time we got off the plane. I ran into a guy named Tone from my neighborhood at a party hosted by Diddy. He asked if he could take me out when we got back to the States. I told him yes and we exchanged numbers. I wasn't committed to anyone. I knew we both had be checking each other out for a while, but never acting on it.

Naj was staying in the same hotel as the rapper Mase and his group, Harlem World. We were at the pool at the same time one day. They asked if I wanted to play water volleyball with them. I couldn't swim, so I was playing around the edge of the pool.

Mase's bodyguard, Cortney, volunteered to teach me to swim. He said he got tired of seeing me just standing on the side of the pool. He taught me in less than an hour. All those years I'd wasted…it was so easy. He said he was a retired Navy Seal, and he invited me to hang out with them the next day at the pool.

All of the guys from the day before were at pool with a few new faces. one of the guys from the group they called "Looney" introduced himself and sat at the swim-up bar talking to me a few other girls. Once he found out I was from Brooklyn, he started mentioning people he knew. I couldn't believe it when he said Damien was his best friend. I burst out laughing and briefly told him about Damien and me.

Cortney was nice, but he wasn't my type. They invited us all to hang-out. I didn't know the other girls, but I was down. We went jet-skiing, and Cortney scared me by going so fast and far out in the ocean. I was annoyed with him and planned to take a cab back to the hotel. Looney must have seen my face because he came to check on me. He said I was fun to be around and asked if we could chill and get to know each other. He didn't know that Naj and I had saw him the day before and thought he was attractive. Looney wanted to ditch the group and so did I. I asked about the girl he was with, he said she was a groupie. We hopped in a cab and left.

We got to the hotel, and I left a note for Naj to let her know how to reach me and who I was with. I stayed with Looney for a few days until he left, then met back up with Naj and the girls on our last night in Mexico. We went to a tequila bar and danced and drank all night. No one warned me about how tequila creeps up on you. By the time we left, I was so drunk I could barely make it to my hotel.

We all headed home the next morning, not feeling well. But we didn't care. Cancun owed us nothing. We'd had the time of our lives.

My dating life after that trip became more complicated. I was unapologetically dating multiple people. I would be in Harlem with Looney some days and other days hanging with my comedian friend Tal. Then, me and Tone started hanging out. I traveled with him out of state a few times after Clayton started going to Florida often.

Dating had become a sport for me. I had lost many battles of the heart, and I wasn't willing to take any more heart hits! Some guys I slept with, and some were just there for a good time.

The spiral was creeping up. I was never home. Tyreek would take our daughter for weeks at a time to Delaware if I told him I needed a break. Everything in my life was moving so fast.

TAKEAWAY

Everyone has something in our lives that we wish was better. We all have a forbidden fruit that satisfies our sinful palates with temporary pleasure. It's not always sexual lust. It can be power, addictions, or a person. It's anything that may cause you to disregard, disrespect, kill, steal, or destroy to have it. We all have that tree of life we are warned not to take from. It's to protect us from damage emotionally, physically, and spiritually.

It takes work to change behaviors. I was at a breaking point in my life. I wanted to control my destiny, but I wasn't doing anything to lead me toward it. I was living for a moment of fun and lost my focus on the future I wanted for me and my daughter.

Chapter 24

COME TO JESUS

"YOU WERE MUCH CLOSER"

Artist: Fred Hammond & Radical for Christ

"KEEP THE FAITH"

Artist: Faith Evans

Summer had come. My sister and her boyfriend, who she'd started seeing after leaving Boogie, got married. Pastor Jackson was a friend of her husband and officiated their wedding. We promised him that we would visit his church in Newburgh, New York. One Sunday, I put on a cute mini dress, and that's what we did. It was about a two-hour drive from Brooklyn. The way I was living my life, I needed to take time for God. On the drive up, I discovered my new favorite gospel artist, Fred Hammond. We listened to his newly released CD "Pages of Life." Almost every song spoke to my soul. It was like God had this entire album waiting just for me. I had heard that God will meet you where you are. That day became my road to Damascus.

During the service people were falling out of their seats, speaking in a language I didn't understand. I thought they were faking. I was told it's called heavenly language. Pastor Jackson would say things to people, and they would cry and hit the floor. I became the devil's advocate sitting there. I thought to myself, "Okay, now watch him ask them for money."

Then this happened: Pastor Jackson called my mom up and began to say things to her. Next thing I knew, she was on the floor, her little wedge heels laid out right with her. It shocked me; I knew then that something was different. I wasn't feeling it at all. I didn't want to be put on the spot, but he called me up.

He told me I was going to get married. I would meet someone from my past that I wouldn't remember, but he would remember me. It would be a short courtship and a quick marriage. He went on to say I knew enough people to fill up his church. Again, I was skeptical; anyone could have told him I was a party promoter. He said he saw me in a classroom and at a new job. He went on to say I was called to minister to women.

Lastly, he said, "You've been broken and never cried about it." My tears started flowing out of nowhere. I don't know what happened. I knew then he was speaking the truth. He had no clue about what I had been through. He said, "After today, your life will never be the same." He took his cloak off and placed it on me. The only thing I remember after that was someone helping me to sit in a chair. No lies told, my life started to change gradually after that day.

TAKEAWAY

I had become a danger to myself. Dating men for money, power, respect, and influence. These weren't relationships; they were exchanges. My past had made me a woman who no longer valued her body or her life. Check yourself before you wreck yourself. We often don't want to accept the truth about ourselves and always point fingers at others' flaws. I thought I had a strong sense of self back then. But, in all honesty, I had none. I was just a young girl who was popular and trying to live up to everyone's expectations of me.

Chapter 25

A CHANGE IS COMING

"FOR THE GOOD OF THEM"

Artist: Milton Brunson and The Thompson Community Singers

My relationship with God became personal after that day in Newburgh. My brother-In-Law Cal introduced us to a few people I connected with during my new spiritual journey. I didn't wake up with a completely changed life; it gradually started changing. Pastor Jackson had become part of the family. He took us to another church in Queens, New York. My sister and I would visit. We ended up in a car accident with Pastor Jackon on our way home from a wedding I attended with him. I had a few minor injuries, So, I took sick leave from work for a few weeks.

During that time, I was trying to attend church. I started slowing down and gradually stop seeing everyone. Clayton had begun going to Florida often. I started hearing his money wasn't all from the entertainment industry. I asked him about it. He opened up and told me everything about his past, living the street life. It was catching up with him. He shared that the Feds were watching him. I got nervous about that, wondering if they were going to knock on my door one day. I started distancing myself from him.

We had an argument one night after we went on a double date at Mr. Chows. He told his friends date I couldn't drive any of his cars with no license. I felt that was none of her business, he was showing off. The argument led to him driving me to a place called Adam's Driving

School on Fulton Street to start the process for my driver's license the next day. He dropped me off on his way to catch a flight back to Florida. He was building a house there and invited me to move there with him. He said if I got my license, he would buy me a car. I was no fool; I wasn't taking anything from him after he told me the Feds were on him.

I was changing spiritually and didn't realize it was happening. The day Clayton dropped me at the driving school became the day that would change my life forever.

I walked into the driving school and saw my homeboy, Pooch. Sitting across the room was another guy who was very handsome. Light skin, with waves in his hair, nice facial features. He looked really young. I didn't think anything of him other than him being some eye candy while I was in the class. We started having a casual conversation. I didn't catch his name, but he told me he was from Lafayette Gardens housing projects, also in Bed-Stuy. I told him I knew a few people from there who attended our parties and ski trips. He mentioned he had heard about an upcoming ski trip and wanted to come.

He chilled with me and Pooch during the break, and after, we took the test we needed to pass the class. Pooch and I finished the exam first, then I took the exam from the other guy and answered all his questions for him. Once we got out of the class, I told the him I hoped to see him on the ski trip and left.

My relationships weren't the only things changing in my life. After I returned to work after the car accident, my boss became very nasty toward me. She was looking for a reason to complain about anything, but I wasn't having it. One thing I knew for certain was that wherever I worked, I brought value. I always tried to create a fun work environment while getting all my work done. Everyone else was glad I was back, even the physicians. She was the only one who'd changed. I figured it was because they'd had no one to cover me while I was out.

One day, she yelled at me in front of patients and threatened termination. That was all I needed. I responded with, "Don't talk to me like that. I'm not your child!" I saw the writing on the wall. The staff had my back, but I knew my mouth and temper. I was a young black receptionist working for a prestigious hospital and a white woman from England who didn't respect me. I was not willing to walk on eggshells to keep that job.

I started searching for a new job. I found a listing for Brooklyn Hospital and called to find out if they had any positions that I qualified for from my work experience. They had a position for a secretary for the Department of Surgery. I immediately applied. It was time for new beginnings across the board.

TAKEAWAY

God is in the midst of it all. No matter where you are in your life, God will get his message to you by any means necessary. I was skeptical about going to that church, but I am so glad I did. Keeping that promise would become one of the best things that I had done for myself in a while.

We all should find something or someone that inspires us to be better. For me, it was my spirituality. It made me look at my life and begin to realize I wasn't living a healthy lifestyle. I wanted to take my Christianity seriously. I knew I couldn't clean up my act by myself. My life was damaged by lust, lies, and deceit. God was the only one I trusted to clean me up.

Chapter 26

PROFESSIONAL GROWTH

"MY LIFE"

Artist: Mary J. Blige

Within two weeks, I had an interview for the position at Brooklyn Hospital. This position even paid more money. There were three interviews to go through in order to get hired. I was offered the position as a secretary for an oncologist surgeon, Dr. Morales. I asked them to give me two weeks to give notice at my current job. They agreed.

My manager looked shocked that I had gotten a position at another hospital so quickly. I had no problem resigning from one of the best hospitals in the country. The staff gave me a farewell party with many well wishes.

I was so excited to finally land a job in Brooklyn. It was another step up in my career. I had to get in and learn quickly, and the other secretaries were so helpful. They embraced me and taught me a lot, especially my girl Candy. She was the secretary to the chief of the department. We got along well from day one. I started in November 1998. It was around the holidays, and we had a few office parties. It allowed me to get to know everyone in a more relaxed environment.

The department had a Christmas party at Terrace on the Park. Everyone looked beautiful and was having a wonderful time. I hadn't gotten the chance to meet with the chief, Dr. Douglas, until that evening. He was a Black West Indian man. Our first encounter was strange. He gave me a very flirtatious compliment about my attire. I brushed it off and just thought I may have taken it the wrong way since he was the boss. I went on to enjoy the evening.

After the holidays and the New Year, I was pretty settled into my position and getting the work done. But things began to become uncomfortable for me with Dr. Douglas. He was always cordial around the staff and his secretary, so I figured he was just a nice, chill man until one morning when I happened to get on the elevator at the same time as him. He grabbed my hand and rubbed the middle of it with his finger. I knew what that meant: Men would do that as a sign of wanting to sleep with a woman. He told me I was a beautiful Black woman and didn't release my hand right away. I thanked him and couldn't wait until the elevator door opened. I felt so disrespected.

I couldn't bring myself to tell my girl Candy. He was everyone's boss, doctors included. I didn't say a word to anyone at first. I tried to avoid him. I went home and told my mom about it. She didn't like it one bit. She advised me to say something. But I was scared because I was new, and I needed my job. The times I couldn't avoid him, he would say inappropriate things to me in passing and make sounds like "um-um-um" while walking behind me. I was slim and curvy, but he had no right to make gestures.

It was becoming blatant sexual harassment. I expected a level of professionalism from a man with so much power. After a few times, I couldn't take it anymore, so I shared it with two of the senior secretaries I thought I could trust. One advised me to start a paper trail of the encounters. They also said they would pay closer attention.

They both eventually witnessed it at different times. They couldn't believe what they heard and saw. I was relieved to know I had witnesses that I may eventually need. Once he realized I wasn't entertaining his gestures, he began to complain about my doctor, which led to complaints about me.

The worst part was when Dr. Morales started being distant with me. He was told that I'd reported him as coming into work intoxicated. I had heard he had some issues with alcohol due to the pressure of his divorce, but I didn't care about that. I'm loyal to my people. If you're good to me, I got you. This had to come from another secretary, not me. I told him I would never do that, but I don't think he trusted me, since I was new.

I was called into the administrator's office. I thank God my administrator was a fair woman and was not blinded by her position. When she told me about the complaints, I confessed to her about everything I had experienced. I told her I had a paper trail along with other witnesses. I also mentioned how it was very convenient that all these complaints had started coming against me and my doctor once I chose to ignore the chief's unprofessional behavior. She understood exactly where I was coming from. I don't think I was the first, and wouldn't be the last, to complain about being treated like that by him. She told me to be careful and do my job. From that day on, I watched and wrote down everything.

Mid-January, on a Saturday, my mom came to pick me up. I had just checked my mail. I had a letter from the NYPD. I was nervous, wondering what they could want with me. I knew I hadn't done anything wrong, but I *had* dealt with men who were heavy in the streets for years. I opened the letter, and it was from the NYPD Department of Investigations informing me that I had been selected as a candidate to become a Correction Officer for the City of New York. I was taken aback. I had taken the test in 1996 when the officers had told me about the job while I'd been visiting Teddy. I hadn't thought anything about it since that day. But this letter came at the right time.

I called and got the process started. I met my investigator, Mrs. Brown, who gave me a packet with specific instructions and a deadline to return it to her. That packet asked for a lot of information, including questions about family members. I remember not wanting to add my brother's name because of his criminal history, along with Tyreek's.

I went to work and shared the news with my co-workers. They couldn't believe I was considering law enforcement. A few of the girls helped me type out my packet. All I thought about was providing a better life for my daughter and getting away from that creep of a doctor. Law enforcement had good benefits and pay, and my mom, who'd just started seeing the man named Aaron who would later become my stepdad, could watch my daughter most of the time. She was four and in pre-K.

After three months of running back and forth to submit paperwork, I got the call to report to the academy on April 1, 1999. I couldn't believe I got the job. I told everyone close to me and gave the hospital my notice. I was given another farewell luncheon.

I needed a driver's license to become a correction officer. Thank God I started the process the day Clayton dropped me off at the driving school. I took my road test and got my license. I called Tyreek with the news, and he gave me a crash course about jail and how to protect myself when I started. I asked Ty to take our daughter for a while after her birthday, which was coming up in a few weeks. I needed to get ready for the academy and didn't want to worry about a babysitter.

During my investigation, I had gotten a call from an old friend, Monz. He was the brother-in-law of Mr. Charles, the school aide at my high school. We had been cool since Mr. Charles introduced us in my freshman year. He'd been in jail but had just come home. We never dated previously, we just hooked up here and there. I was single; no one was checking for me, and I wasn't checking for them. He started coming around more, and we fell into an unexpected relationship that I wasn't looking for at the time. He said he wasn't going back to jail. He wanted to change his life around.

I cared for Monz, but I should have never started a relationship with him with everything I had going on. He was comfortable and familiar, and I took that for granted. I just wanted something constant. He was always solid, and I didn't have to figure him out, since I had known him and his family for years.

One of my homegirls, Nakia, had also started her process as a correction officer, so we started together. Shock Day was crazy. The PT instructors were no joke; they didn't crack a smile. I don't shake easily, but the way they were yelling in our faces I felt their drops of saliva on me. I wasn't sure if I was going to show up the following Monday. I thought I was cute with my ponytail and red lipstick. They made it loud and clear not to come back there with jewelry or makeup. Me and Nakia were both nervous, but happy. She picked me up every day to get to the academy. We ended up in the same company squad.

We needed specific equipment, and it was expensive. I didn't have money like that. I had bills living on my own. Monz hadn't been home long enough to help, and besides, I wasn't going to rekindle anything with anyone for the money. I was stressed trying to figure out how I was going to get the money. It was too short notice for my parents. It was the top of the month, and everyone had bills to pay. Out of the blue, Tone called me. I was surprised to hear from him. It had been about four months since I'd seen or spoken to him, before my birthday in December. He stopped by to give me money for my birthday and Christmas after missing my party. He was like that, even after we decided to be friends.

He asked what I was doing, and I told him about starting the academy. He was happy for me. I told him I didn't know if I could do it because of the uniform and equipment expenses. He wouldn't hear that as an excuse. He asked how much I needed, and he gave me the money right there. He was happy to see someone he knew doing it right and asked if I needed anything else, to let him know. I thanked him and he left. God showed up through a friend without a sexual exchange. I was ready for my new beginnings as a NYC Department of Corrections recruit.

TAKEAWAY

You may not know a change is coming in your life due to unforeseen circumstances or an unexpected blessing. Always work hard to position yourself for change. Embrace every steppingstone and you could step up into new opportunities. I always made room for professional growth. I wasn't afraid to use my skills and learn something new.

Chapter 27

OTHER SIDE OF THE GATE

"MIDST OF IT ALL"

Artist: Yolanda Adams

I was flowing through the Correction Academy and meeting some nice people. My daughter turned five. We had a small birthday party at my apartment, and a few of my classmates from the academy were invited. Tyreek and I took Nu-Nu and my nephew EJ to Coney Island Amusement Park together to celebrate with her before he took her to Delaware with him so I could focus on getting through the academy.

During my time in the academy, one of my aunts passed away. My dad's sister and Cousin Mena's mom, Hattie. She had been on life support for a few weeks after having a stroke. I was very close to her. Monz was by my side through it all.

Me and my sister Lee started going to a church in Queens on Tuesday evenings. I no longer wanted to party as much on the weekend. I was understanding the Bible more and learning how to pray for myself. The pastor of the church kept it real in his sermons. He understood we were not the average church girls. He was very delicate with us. I tried buying clothes that I felt were appropriate for church. The pastor even gave me a compliment one Sunday.

My life was changing for the better. I would no longer be visiting people in jail or prison. I felt accomplished. No one helped me get there. No referrals, like my previous jobs. I was starting a career that looked very different from the lifestyle I had been living. This was the turning point for me, an opportunity to learn and see life with a fresh set of eyes. I deserved it, and I refused to do anything to ruin it for myself. I was locked in to becoming a correction officer. I would no longer just be "the party girl," or "the girl with all the broken relationships," or "the college dropout." This was the beginning of me changing the mindsets of my peers. They would then know that they could change things in their lives and do whatever it was they put their minds to, just as I did.

Monz asked me to marry him after my aunt passed away. I said yes too soon without thinking about everything. I was still grieving my aunt and wasn't in the right mental space. I questioned myself. Was I completely done with Damien or with Clayton? Was I in love with Monz, or was he just comforting to my heart? He was my friend, and I didn't want to hurt him. But I had to choose me. I knew I had to do the right thing by breaking things off.

I was honest, telling Monz about my concerns that his criminal past could cost me the job. He accepted my choice to end things. He was not a weak man who would have begged me to try to make it work. He took it and moved on. I am glad to say he eventually forgave me and is still my homie. He's doing well for himself. I know that any woman he is with is blessed.

It was finally graduation day after three long months of hard work and para-military training. My family and closest friends were there to support me. I had done it! I was going to jail! This time, not to visit anyone but as a correction officer. I could have never imagined this for my life. My first assignment was the Rose M. Singer female detention center. Most rookie female officers did not want to be assigned to that command. I didn't care. Nakia also went to the same facility. They had us on opposite schedules. This meant I had to get transportation to work. That didn't take long. One of my classmates had the same tour as me for a while, and she would pick me up. I always gave her money for gas.

It was scary and different. The unknown. I worked "the wheel" four days on and two days off. Midnights, evenings, and days. I loved working there. I met some of my closest friends to date at Rosie's. I also found out the truth about Damien, finally. I told him he might as well tell me because I was not going to be a secret to anyone after Nakia heard he had a wife who was also an officer.

He called one night and told me everything. He was, in fact, married and did have a child. He told me he was separated when we met and didn't think our relationship was going to move as fast as it did. He had no plans to fall in love with me, but he did. He also said she was a good woman, and he thought getting married would make him a better man. Obviously, it hadn't. Those times we spent nights together had to be the times they were on the outs.

Once he got his truth out, he came around a lot to prove he only wanted me. I wanted to hurt him the way he hurt me. I continued to sleep with him for my own pleasure for a while. I got pregnant by him and decided to have an abortion. He tried to convince me to keep the baby and said that we could make it work. I wasn't buying it.

I wanted none of that for my life. I especially didn't want someone else's husband. He couldn't do much of anything for me. After that last abortion, I was running to the church so much that I had my co-worker Nessa going with me. We had become so close in a short amount of time. I was reflecting on what I had become over the years.

I had found myself trying to use guys to distract me from Damien, especially after I continued to sleep with him for months, even knowing he was married. I never wanted to be that girl.

As much as I was connecting with my own spirituality, it didn't completely stop me from going back to my coping mechanisms when I felt stress: partying and men. One day, my bro Ray from Ugly Productions called me. He was concerned after one of our parties when a few guys I was dating showed up. Damien came with his artist, and a guy named Ski was there. I was running around with him, my boy Heav (R.I.P), and the boxer Zab. I told Ski I didn't want a relationship, but we could hang out. My boys covered for me. Ray told me I was playing a dangerous game, knowing the guys that had feelings for me were no suckers; they were men with egos. He said I was going to eventually get myself or someone else hurt, and they weren't going to be able to protect me.

He was right, and I knew it. I had disregarded everything I knew to be right. That moment was the final turning point. I had to focus on being the only parent for my daughter. Tyreek caught a case in Delaware during my probation period with the job. I had to report it to the department. He wasn't able to contact me directly for a long time due to their phone restrictions.

I realized that a lot of the female officers had similar life experiences as me from growing up in the hood and no longer wanted that lifestyle for themselves. We did the job with gratitude. I walked into those jails every day, knowing I had so many people I cared about in a prison or jail. I could have easily been on the other side of the prison gate because of the people I associated with.

I watched and paid attention to everything the senior officers said and did. I started riding to work with another officer named Griffy. It didn't last long. I worked with her for one week, and she was being mean to the inmates and didn't like how they were more receptive to me. I was trying to help her, as the senior officer advised us to work as a team. I heard her talking about me to a few work detail inmates. That was a big no-no! I heard her and cursed her out. I had to call Damien that day to pick me up, and I knew I had to get a car quickly.

God kept showing up for me. My bestie Tash had a red Chevy Nova that her aunt had given to her to commute when she was in college. She sold it to me for five hundred dollars. I no longer had to depend on anyone for a ride to work.

After a year, I was transferred from Rosie's to the Anna M. Kross Center (AMKC) male facility. I had bought a more reliable car, a used, pearl-colored Nissan Altima. I loved that car and only had it a few months before it was stolen near Rikers. I was working the evening tour and parked on the street to get a ride across the bridge to the jail. I got off work, and the car was gone. When they found it a week later, it was completely stripped. Insurance paid and claimed it was a total loss. I went back to my old faithful Chevy Nova.

One misconception most civilians have about Rikers Island is that it is one big jail. It's not. There are multiple facilities and jails within the city. The department had transferred a lot of new officers to other facilities; they didn't have to give an explanation why, either. It was like starting all over again. It was very intimidating. Thank God the officers at AMKC made sure the female officers were safe and taught me how to work with male inmates. I was only there for two months before I got transferred again, this time to Otis Bantum Correctional Center (OBCC). It was a punitive segregation facility. From the time I walked in, a lot of my co-workers were telling me how horrible it was working punitive segregations at "The Bing". The inmates were housed there as disciplinary actions for violent behavior or being caught with contraband. I hated working there and was upset that I had been transferred for no reason.

The newer officers were always the ones to be transferred to facilities that needed more staff, but I was no longer one of the newest members of service. There was a class that came on in 2000. I made a few calls with my concerns, one to the union and one to the Guardian Association representative at the academy. The union did come to address my concerns, and the president at the time found my complaints to be valid. The rep from the Guardians never got back to me.

I had met some good, solid people in my short amount of time on the job. I met an officer named Kevin Lynah during my annual job training at the academy, and he became a mentor and brother to me. He worked at the Brooklyn Detention Center. He introduced me to his boy, Michael Grays. They told me to meet them in Harlem at the Guardian's monthly meeting to share my concerns, and I did. I explained that I was a single mom who had been unfairly transferred twice in two months. My record was good, and I had taken no days off.

I also shared what my classmates told me about the treatment of the new and female officers in The Bing at the time. A civilian worker, Father Lucas, worked there as well and happened to be at that meeting. He vouched for what I shared. After the meeting, a lot of people were handing me cards and telling me to reach out to them if I needed assistance with anything. A few days later, I received a call from Kev. "We took care of you lil' sis." I didn't know what he meant, but I thanked him.

They fought hard for women and men of color in law enforcement to be treated fairly. It was no secret that there was systematic racism within law enforcement. He told me a friend of theirs, Eric, was a member of an organization called 100 Blacks in Law Enforcement. Eric made a phone call to the Guardians about me as well. I was blown away by the support of three Black men who had no relationship with me, fighting for me.

I never met their friend Eric, but I was grateful for his concern. Years later, that same friend, Eric Adams, became the Brooklyn Borough President and the second Black Mayor of New York City in 2021.

I went back to work at OBCC. It was the last day of the month, and my girl, Dawny from Marcy, was working in the control room. She called me and informed me I had been transferred to Brooklyn House of Detention (BKDC), the facility where Kev and Mike worked. I was shocked.

On the first day at BKDC, I felt I belonged there, just like I had at Rosie's and AMKC. Brooklyn was much busier than the facilities on Rikers. It was an old jail without the electric cell door functions. The officers there were like one big family. They taught me how to work posts that most new officers never saw until they had more time on the job.

I was still under a lot of stress in my personal life. Tyreek was facing some serious jail time. My mom had felt the need for a change and moved to Detroit. Meanwhile, my sister and I did our best to work and take care of our kids.

TAKEAWAY

When you witness people taking advantage of their power and authority, speak up. When you're not part of the solution, you become part of the problem. I wanted to be treated fairly. Sometimes, speaking up for yourself may come with a cost. After having felt silenced before, it is a cost I have always been willing to pay. I knew I was always going to use my voice for what was right. My speaking up helped me and other officers who wouldn't speak up for themselves.

Chapter 28

THE BREAKING FOR THE MAKING

"A ROSE IS STILL A ROSE"

Artist: Aretha Franklin

I started feeling like I was living a double life. I was becoming more spiritually conscious and disciplined with how I spent my time due to the job. Then I would become the reckless party girl. The job changed me for the better while God was being patient with me.

In late 2000 to early 2001, I tried to work fewer days. We were allowed to change our work shifts with one another to extend days off or take days off other than vacation time. I was so overwhelmed and disappointed with myself. My mom was in Detroit, and my cousin Ken was pregnant, so I was going to the "D" once a month. I had even met a guy there named Raymond, who was a singer-songwriter. We connected through music. I told him about my daughter singing songs she would make up. He took her in the studio at four years old to record the song she said she had written called "Hey boy". Don't ask me what a four-year-old knew about a boy.

I kept reminding myself I needed a change for the better. I needed my family, and I needed to make sure my daughter was good. I'd been telling her Tyreek was away at school instead of in jail. After I found out how much jail time he had received, I had to accept the fact that he wouldn't be around to raise her with me.

I wasn't making a lot of extra money by promoting parties anymore, and I had bills that were behind. I had horrible spending habits. If I wanted something, I bought it. I was one of those mothers who had my phone bill in my daughter's name to avoid paying my old bill. I did everything the hood taught me to do to survive. It's ridiculous looking back at the things I thought were okay because I had friends who were doing it. My mom never would have done that. I could have gotten the money to pay my bills from anyone I was dating, but I never wanted them to think I needed them to take care of us financially. I was disappointed in myself for so many reasons and was drained from my work tour changes.

I was even thinking about leaving the job and moving to another state for a fresh start. I should not have made my last trip to Detroit for the holidays in 2000. I knew I was behind on my rent and had received an eviction notice. I tried to get a court date on the calendar, but the judge denied the request. My building's new management didn't like me and wanted to get rid of me. I mailed in my rent checks before I left for Michigan in the hope things would be good when I returned. That didn't happen.

While I was in Detroit for the holidays, bringing in New Year's 2001, I received a call from Patty. She sounded frantic and informed me that I was being evicted. My mom heard her and started questioning me about it. She didn't like what she was hearing at all. It was happening as a result of my negligence. I felt like God had been patient with me, but now he was dealing with me on another level. I remained calm as Patty told me they were packing up my furniture.

I had recently prayed to God to take away the things I was doing that were destructive to myself, especially my lustful nature. I wanted to be cleansed from my sinful lifestyle. That apartment was tainted with lust. I would even give my keys to my friends when I was away so they could bring guys or girls there to have sex. God was removing everything he could in order to save my life.

I wanted more for myself, and that eviction was the eye-opener I needed! I began to ask God for forgiveness like never before. I knew I was empty and damaged. I was walking around, living like a frame without a picture in it. I felt like I was damaged, used goods, and old garbage.

I called my sister and asked if I could stay with her for a little while until I found another apartment. I didn't plan to stay long. She was fine with it as long as I had my own phone line (she knew we both liked to talk). I had it installed, and I also had a cellphone—it was the beginning of text messaging. I moved it with her once I returned from Detroit.

Damien was the only one who knew I was living with my sister and was looking for an apartment. He never asked what happened. I just told him that I needed a bigger place. He told me that his friend had an apartment for rent in his brownstone. I took that into consideration.

I was at work on the evening shift and felt sick. I noticed I was bleeding, though I'd already had my monthly cycle. I informed my supervisor, and they took me to the hospital. I notified my sister, and she told my mom. My mom and Ken came to New York immediately. The doctors couldn't find anything major, though they did see a cyst. I took a few days off and, after that, felt fine. I guess the stress had affected my body physically.

Ken went back home, but Mommy stayed, and we were happy about that. My sister and I both needed her; she always held us accountable. I went with my mom to check out Damien's friend's place, a duplex apartment in his brownstone. It was beautiful. He offered it to me for almost nothing. Mommy loved the apartment and was going to stay there with me. After we left, she was excited, but I immediately had a spiritual awakening moment. I hated to disappoint her, but it felt like God was warning me not to take it. He revealed to me that I would never be able to break off things permanently with Damien if I stayed in his friend's house. I knew the difference by then when my mind was telling me something, and when God was. I had to adhere to what I heard. I obeyed God and didn't take it.

While staying with my sister, everything was happening for the better. I went out partying at the clubs a couple of times with my childhood friends, Lady and Meka. One night, I got a call from the disappearing act Clayton. I thought maybe the Feds had caught him. I had only seen him a couple of times after I started the job. I told him I needed a watch for work, and he brought me a Movado. I told him a regular watch, as I said he did everything over the top.

He told me he was in town and wanted to come see me. I didn't tell him I was living with my sister for two reasons: I was embarrassed, and I also didn't want him to do anything for me. So, instead, I lied and told him I wasn't feeling well and went out with the girls to a club on Houston Street. Meka's boyfriend worked there as a bouncer. He escorted us upstairs to the V.I.P. We were having a good time just chilling. I was looking over the balcony when I felt a smack on my butt. All I thought before turning around was, "Dang, we are going to have a fight tonight!". But before I could turn around fully, I heard, "You don't look sick to me." I was busted. I just laughed.

Clayton asked me why I lied. I told him they begged me to come out. I also told him it was because of his behavior. He started talking to me about us. They were leaving, and Lady wanted us to leave with them. They had rooms at a hotel near the airport. I explained to her it wasn't like that with Clayton and me anymore.

But I was glad we left with them. Clayton and I were able to have a vulnerable and honest conversation about our relationship. He never understood why I would never fully commit to him or want to start a family with him. He controlled everything and everyone around him. I reminded him of the day he'd told me if I got pregnant, he was going to buy me a house and move me out of my apartment. That was a trigger for me. All I heard was, "I will control you if you get pregnant." Having the Feds on his back was another problem.

We weren't intimate that evening. We made amends and fell asleep. He left money for me on the nightstand before leaving again for Florida. That was the last time I saw him for a few years. For a brief moment that night, I considered quitting my job and letting him take care of us since I had no place of my own. That thought went away quickly. God was covering my mind.

Valentine's Day was a couple of weeks later. Damien came by and wanted to take me out. I didn't want to go anywhere, but I didn't want us to be hanging out in my sister's apartment. I told him to drive to downtown Brooklyn, to Juniors Restaurant. I didn't say anything to him, but I was bothered he'd come to take me out for Valentine's Day when he still had a wife. We'd only made it halfway downtown to the restaurant when I asked him to take me back home. I told him that as long as he had a wife, I could never be a wife, and I no longer wanted to be with him. He was very calm. I was pissed at his demeanor of "Okay, cool." He told me if it wasn't me, it would be someone else.

I kept thinking about what would happen if I became someone like her. If she was such a beautiful person, how could he handle her that way? He was selfish and a liar. He hurt me and was hurting another woman he'd committed to legally. He turned his car around and dropped me back off. He called me a few days later to discuss everything again. He wanted to go to talk, and I agreed to hear what he wanted to say since he was so unbothered before.

We ate, talked, and even slept together. I slept with him intentionally as my final goodbye. I knew if I truly wanted a new life in Christ, breaking up with him was non-negotiable. Years later, he eventually got a divorce. We never got back together, but I did forgive him. He also gave me a sincere apology. We remain cordial all these years later. I knew I had made my mistake and wanted to be forgiven, so I extended that grace to him. No one is perfect.

TAKEAWAY

Don't let lust rob you of your moral values. I did what was right in the wrong situation. The end result is real simple: you reap what you sow in love and life. I dragged out a relationship with a man who I knew was lying to me. The signs were there. I didn't hurt anyone but myself. Don't displace what you are feeling. If you choose to accept what you find out, be ready to live with that choice. I knew the things I valued and respected. Marriage was at the top of my list.

Chapter 29

THE V.I.P FOR ME

Song: "REMARKABLE"

Artist: Jaheim

On February 17, three days after breaking things off with Damien, Lady and Meka stopped by. Lady wanted me to go to a birthday celebration for one of her friends in the city. Although I wasn't in the mood to party, I went. My mother told me to go, and she would babysit.

Once we arrived, we were escorted to the V.I.P. section. I saw a bunch of extremely tall guys and a few celebrities that were there for Lady's homegirl. My Ugly Production Brother Milk was there with an NBA player named Lamar Odom and his entourage. Milk offered to introduce me to a few players. I declined and told him I wasn't into basketball players. He came back and told me someone wanted to meet me. The guy was nice and was Odom's right-hand man. I told him no, but he begged me to let him introduce me to the guy. I finally agreed. He came back with this light-skinned guy around six-foot-one, who was smiling from ear to ear. I don't think I cracked a smile. He offered to buy me a drink. We went to the bar and talked briefly. He introduced himself and told me they called him "Pumpkin". I thought that was a funny name for a grown man. I asked him for his real name, and he told me Anthony. We exchanged numbers. I didn't think anything of it, especially after I saw him talking to a group of girls. I wasn't trying to give him any more energy that night.

I reached home and had a voice message from him. I knew I wasn't going to be calling him "Pumpkin." I just called him "P." He'd wanted to make sure I got home safely. I thought that was sweet. We began to talk on the phone daily. We weren't able to see each other because of my work schedule, but he made me laugh every time we talked. I hadn't laughed in a long time. He was from the Lafayette Gardens housing projects in Brooklyn, but going back and forth to L.A.

One night, I was headed to work for the midnight tour. He told me he'd cooked some food, and he had a plate for me. I met him at Dekalb and Franklin Avenue and took the food to work. I was scheduled to work with my boy, Officer Jermont. He always looked out for me if I needed assistance with anything. I told him about P's cooking for me. There was fried chicken, Kraft mac and cheese, and broccoli. He even gave me a slice of chocolate cake. Jermont said he seemed like a good guy, and I should give him a shot.

My weekend off was coming up, so P and I set a date to go to the movies that Friday. Just my luck it was freezing, and my car had been towed for parking tickets. I took the G train to him on my way back from an office party at my old job on 59th Street, where I'd done medical billing. P came down to meet me at the bodega across the street from his building. He bought something there and told me he had to get back upstairs since he was babysitting his younger brother and cousins. I hoped he wasn't going to leave minors alone while we went to the movies.

This was my first time in Lafayette Gardens. My hangout had been Marcy Houses. These buildings had twenty floors. He lived on the fourteenth. When we got to his apartment, it was warm and cozy. The kids were running around having fun in the back. I got random calls from Clayton and Damien that night, but I never answered.

P had all my attention. He had a smile to light up a room. I hadn't noticed how handsome he was the other night at the club. Everything felt just right. His demeanor was so different. I had never met anyone from the hood who was so calm and peaceful. I felt the weight of the world I had been carrying being lifted the longer I sat with him.

He told me his dad lived there with him and how he had plans to move to L.A permanently. I was upset. Why had I met someone who was moving across the country? But I just made the best of the night. We couldn't go to the movies since it was late, and the kids were there. I told him about my car, and he said he would go with me to pick it up. He offered to let me stay the night because it was freezing outside. I felt comfortable enough to stay.

The next morning, I woke up to breakfast. I slept like a baby. We spent the entire weekend together, going to get my car and shopping for a gift for him to take to a baby shower. I just kept saying to myself, "This is too good to be true." I was thinking he must be horrible sexually or something. There is no way he was that fine, smelled good, had his own apartment, had a great personality, and was funny with no girlfriend. Maybe this was just his "honeymoon stage" personality. The only thing he didn't have was a car. I didn't care. I was just glad he wasn't a hustler. I may have hit the jackpot.

Everything about him was perfect to me. The way he touched me felt pure and sensual at the same time. I didn't know he smoked weed until I went to his house in the daytime, but I didn't care about that. He would have a house full of guys watching sports, playing PlayStation, and smoking.

After being with him every day for about two weeks, he told me that he'd met me before. I asked where, figuring it was a party or trip. He said he'd met me at the defensive driving course almost two years prior. I sat up, my life flashing in front of me. I was bugging out. "Omg, I took your test for you! You told me you wanted to come to the ski trip." He smiled and said yes, that was him.

That night at the club, he'd known it was me. It was why he'd asked Milky to introduce him to me. That made me fall even more for him.

Even though he wanted to move to L.A., we decided to be together as a couple. I wanted to be with him all day, every day. Anyone I ever I thought I loved, didn't feel like I felt after such a short time with P. It was time for him to meet my family.

He spent a night with me at my sister's apartment and met my mom. She told him to take his durag off and said she would not be calling him "Pumpkin," only Anthony. That never happened. He became "Pumpkin" to my entire family. Especially once everyone found out he'd been born on Halloween and his granny had given him that nickname. I began to take my daughter and nephew over to his place a lot. I watched how P and his dad interacted with her. She was very comfortable; if she hadn't been, that would have been a deal breaker.

My mom had gone back to work, so we were tag teaming to get the kids. My stepdad and P had become part of the pick-up crew. Our relationship was moving fast and all for the better. My daughter was hospitalized for her asthma, and I was there all day and night. He came up and stayed with us for a long time. She called him Daddy. I told her not to say that again. He said it was okay, but I was not comfortable with that. I told him she had a dad, and I didn't want him to feel pressured.

After my daughter was released from the hospital, we went over to his apartment to hang out. She was used to being there, and she called his dad "Grandpa." I corrected her again. He told me it was fine, but I wanted her to call him by his name.

I knew how Tyreek felt about her. I always made sure she understood she had her biological dad, and P. I didn't want her to think she couldn't embrace them both.

I also told the fellas I was no longer going to promote parties. I wanted P to get to know me, not the party girl. All I did was spend time with him and my family. I was still going to church, though not as consistently.

P asked me if I wanted to move in with him. I said no. He asked why. He had three bedrooms, and it was just him and his dad. He'd lived in that apartment all his life, except for when he lived with his dad's family in Queens after his mom passed away when he was fourteen. He had started to get in trouble back then. His grandmother never took his name off the lease so that he would always have a place to call home. He decided to take a chance with me and not move to L.A. He told me he loved me, and his actions showed it from the start.

So many people were wondering how things happened so fast between us. He was the only man in my life that had made love easy. We had a connection right away. There was no baby mama or wife drama, no drug dealing, stealing, or robbing, no expectations, and no extensive prison history. If smoking weed and PlayStation were our biggest issues, I would be okay with them.

How could I not love and appreciate what God had done for me? P was just a man who wanted to love a flawed woman like me. A twenty-eight-year-old single mother with a dark past. Once, a young girl who'd found peace in music and dancing. A girl who had been called names because of her dark skin. He chose me because God chose me at birth. He never judged my past. I shared most of my life with him. Some things I had been too embarrassed to share, but I didn't have to second-guess his love for us.

Meeting him that day during the defensive driving class in 1999 was the second-best thing that has ever happened to me.

TAKEAWAY

If you close your heart to love, you close your life to living. Love is worth living for, no matter what it takes to get there. After all the things I had gone through, all the stupid decisions I had made, I was now twenty-eight years old and deciding to accept the mercy God gave me. I allowed my heart the opportunity to learn what love meant and feel its purity. I released the bad that had been in my life to receive what was happening that was good.

Chapter 30

UNAPOLOGETIC LOVE

SONG

"SHOW ME LOVE"

When I had no one to call my own, so brokenhearted and all alone
(You were there) you were there to comfort me
You're my everything, and no one can love me like you do
When I'm down, you show me love
When times get rough, you show me love
When I can't go on, you show me love again
Over and over again

Artist: Tamia

It hadn't been three full months when we confessed our love. I had so many experiences of tainted love and promises. This was beyond different for us. This time, I was experiencing it through a spiritual eye, even though I was still damaged. God gave me a vision differently. He allowed my heart to feel and my mind to process it purely.

P again offered for me to move in with him. My mom told me to do it and save money. She said most men move in on women, and here he was doing the offering. I was skeptical. I had never lived in a housing project, and I hadn't lived with a man since that brief time Riz moved with me. But I followed my mom's advice and moved. He was like the mayor in his housing complex. They showed him so much love, and I received the same after I moved in.

I didn't know P was so popular and had an army of friends. I thought I knew a lot of people. Everywhere I went with him, he knew someone. He wasn't as young as I thought he was that day I first saw him at the driving class. He was twenty-six, just a few years younger than me. He wanted me to meet some of his other family members. His cousin Mandi heard we were dating, and she told me not to hurt her cousin. She knew me from partying and the type of men I'd dated previously. I respected her valid concern and told her I wouldn't – I loved him.

He took me and my daughter to meet his grandmother Val, godmother Linda, and her daughter Leesa. We clicked from day one. I actually knew Linda's oldest daughter. She'd gone to City Kids. The funny thing is, she had dated Mel during the time of all the cheating rumors back in the day. We were so happy to reconnect, and we are sisters now.

After five months of dating, P started talking about marriage. I told him if he ever wanted to ask me to marry him, he would first have to ask my dad. One Saturday, we drove to Jersey to see him. We sat around talking, and out of nowhere, he asked him if he could marry me. My dad said yes, as long as he could take care of us as well as my dad had always done. I was glad to hear that. I figured he would ask me eventually since he now had my dad's approval.

He came into our bedroom one day while I was lying in the bed. He asked me, "Do you want to get married?" I was looking at him like we'd had this conversation numerous times already. I said yes. He pulled out a ring that I had shown him and put it on my finger. I couldn't believe it. We kissed, and I called my mom and sister to tell them the news. I was actually engaged. God reminded me of the prophecy I'd received in 1998 from Pastor Jack. I had met my forever love just like he said I would. I didn't remember P at first, but he'd remembered me. Pastor Jack had said it would be a short courtship and quick marriage. I was engaged within five months of meeting him, but we didn't marry all that quickly. I became his wife two years later, on May 17, 2001. We've been married for over twenty years now! God keeps his promises!

FINAL THOUGHTS AND TAKEAWAY

"THE STORY I TELL"

Artist: Maverick City Music

God favored "The Black Wildflower," and He gave me beauty for ashes. God is love and the mender of broken hearts. Mine started to mend in 2001. I pray that my story is evidence of God's love and forgiveness. Just like the story of Rahab in the Bible, so many people will say, "You can't turn a whore into a housewife." I believe that's a lie. God turned Rahab's life around when she hid the two spies and spared her family from death, and she married into the bloodline of Jesus Christ.

No, I didn't solicit men as a prostitute. But when I gave myself away for anything other than love and marriage, I sold my worth. God restored me. He heard my cries and rescued me from what the world had falsely told me was right and from the things I'd subscribed to and used as survival tactics. We can all be rescued. We just have to want it, and when the help comes, we must take it. My wildflower can bloom now for the world to see. There will be times when I may need some extra watering, and your flower may need some extra watering and attention, too. And that's okay. Blossom flowers! BLOSSOM!

ACKNOWLEDGMENTS

My Lord and Savior Jesus Christ! Your Grace is still sufficient!

To my heartbeats and the reason why I breathe: Anthony, Eboni, and Amari, thank you for always supporting me. Holding my hands and being my biggest cheerleaders. Thank you for allowing me to share my story without shame.

To my mommy Eunice and step-dad Aaron. My daddy Charles and stepmom Barbara: Thank you for every sacrifice you made for me to become the woman I am today.

To Felicia "Lisa" Davis: God blessed me when he chose me to be your big sister!

To my entire family: I'm nothing without you. Especially my babies! Thank you, Earl, Jeanette, and Chrissy, for always keeping me on my toes. Ma Bert, Big Sis Deb and Brother Ted, love you both. Crea, Te'anna, Tezmar, Stephen, I love you, little bro. My Godchildren, Radikal4kidz Inc., and Eboni's friends - my bonus babies. My sister-cousins.

My extended family: Anthony Turner, Linda Lipscomb, Booker, Lipscomb, Washington, Brown, Shider, Sanders, Roper and Spann families. Thank you for always loving me for me.

My Best friends and my homegirls. You have held me down and stood by my side during the darkest moments in my life. If you know, you know!!! Name dropping will get me in trouble! Special shoutout: Pamela, Nikki, Tash, Terri, Vanessa, Charlotte, Jackie, Cynthia, Veronica, Desiree, Latoya and Linette.

My childhood and neighborhood friends: Herkimer Street family, Kingston Avenue, Albany Avenue P.S 93, Satellite III JHS, Paul Robeson H.S, SUNY Old Westbury, Marcy Houses and Lafayette Gardens.

My brothers for life! Maxwell, Raino, Patrice, Bill, IBM dancers and UG Baby!

To my MSU Sisters, Women of Zion, and Prayer warriors. Thank you for every prayer, word of encouragement, hug, and listening ear.

My NYC Department of Correction Family: We are the Boldest!

My social media Jolly Ranchers: Thanks for supporting me always!

May my angels rest peacefully: Nanny and Pops, Big Gram, Aunts: Hattie and Liz, Grandma Val, Uncle Mike, Uncle Chicken, Unique, Priest Lamel "Showtime" Lawson, Eugene Jonah Roper, Rayfield, and Stephanie Booker.

Patricia Wooster – Thank you for holding my hand to the finish line.

Happy Self-Publishing – Thank you for your patience and professionalism.

This book is dedicated to every child being raised in underserved communities all over the world.

ABOUT THE AUTHOR

PASTOR TINA BOOKER is a distinguished individual with a wealth of experience and expertise. She brings a rich background encompassing a career in law enforcement, entrepreneurship, and pastoral leadership. With over two decades of dedicated service, she has demonstrated a profound commitment to helping individuals tap into their unique gifts, talents, and abilities to achieve remarkable success.

Pastor Booker's professional journey extends beyond her law enforcement career. She is an accomplished entrepreneur, motivational speaker, and ministry leader. Through her non-profit organizations, Faith House Ministries and Radikal4kidz Inc., she has made substantial contributions to community outreach, mainly focusing on providing valuable resources to children in underserved communities and addressing the mass incarceration crisis in inner-city areas.

One of her notable achievements is establishing the annual "Melanin Magic Gala" in New York City, celebrating the accomplishments and achievements of women of color. She is also recognized as a co-collaborator of the "Female Entrepreneur Playbook," a collaborative guide for women entrepreneurs. Additionally, she has collaborated with her husband on "Built to Build: Doing Business God's Way with Your Spouse or Partner," aimed at supporting entrepreneurs and small businesses.

Pastor Booker's dedication and service have been recognized through numerous awards, citations, and acknowledgments within the Department of Corrections and in her broader community. Her expertise extends to High Impact Empowerment Coaching, where she empowers women to unlock their full potential through her "Built to Build" consulting and mentoring program. Her ministry work encompasses powerful worship services that deliver biblical truths in relevant and practical ways, infused with God's love.

Beyond her professional pursuits, Pastor Tina Booker is a devoted wife, mother, and grandmother. Her unwavering dedication, compassion, and leadership continue to inspire those who have the privilege of knowing her. Her guiding motto is, "I just want God to be pleased with my service to His people."

Contact her on:
Instagram: https://www.instagram.com/Tinabooker_official
Facebook: https://www.facebook.com/pastortinab
LinkedIn: https://www.linkedin.com/in/tina-booker-7313967a?utm
Website: https://eztree.me/TINABOOKER

THANKS

Thank You For Reading My Book!

I really appreciate all of your feedback, and I love hearing what you have to say.

I need your input to make the next version of this book and my future books even better.

Please leave me a helpful review on Amazon letting me know what you thought of the book.

Thank you so much!
Tina M. Booker

Happy Self Publishing is a one-stop destination for publishing services such as book cover design, editing, formatting, audiobook narration, website design, and marketing. At Happy Self Publishing we help authors find their voice and self-publish professionally.

► **WHAT WE DO:** We help coaches, consultants, trainers, speakers, and entrepreneurs who aspire to position themselves as the trusted experts in their field by helping them become bestselling authors within 6 months or less, even if they hate writing.

► **HOW WE DO IT:** We show you how to build a profitable author funnel and use the book as the lead magnet in the funnel to give you expert positioning and attract qualified leads for your business.

► **WHY IT WORKS:** After working with over 400 authors from 35 countries, we've been able to simplify the process and show you the easiest and fastest way to publish your book. It doesn't matter at what stage of your author journey you are currently - we have the tools & resources to take you to the next step and help you publish a world-class book.

► **SERVICES WE PROVIDE:**

✓ book writing aka angel writing
✓ book coaching
✓ editing
✓ book cover design
✓ formatting
✓ publishing ebooks, paperback & audiobooks
✓ global distribution
✓ author websites
✓ book trailers
✓ bestseller promotions

www.happyselfpublishing.com
writetous@happyselfpublishing.com

Schedule a free Book Strategy
Call with us to discuss your book project:
www.happyselfpublishing.com/call

Made in the USA
Middletown, DE
04 January 2025